Biography of
a Chairman
Mao Badge

Biography of a Chairman Mao Badge

The Creation and Mass Consumption of a Personality Cult

Melissa Schrift

Rutgers University Press

New Brunswick, New Jersey, and London

Library of Congress Cataloging-in-Publication Data

Schrift, Melissa, 1968–
    Biography of a Chairman Mao badge : the creation and
mass consumption of a personality cult / Melissa Schrift.
      p. cm.
    Includes bibliographical references and index.
    ISBN 0–8135–2936–0 (cloth : alk. paper) — ISBN 0–8135–2937–9
(pbk. : alk. paper)
    1. Mao, Tse-tung, 1893–1976—Medals. 2. Badges—China. Title.

DS778.M3 S343 2001
951.05'092—dc21   00–045895

British Cataloging-in-Publication data for this book is available from
the British Library.

Manufactured in the United States of America

To my boys, Keith, Cameron, and Quinn

Contents

Acknowledgments

Among others, I am particularly grateful to the members of the anthropology graduate program at the University of Hawaii–Manoa who allowed me the creative space to conceptualize a doctoral research project focused on the somewhat offbeat topic of Mao badges. I am deeply grateful for the intellectual support, flexibility, and faith shown by Fred Blake, Nina Etkin, Jocelyn Linnekin, Ruth Dawson, Alan Howard, and Christine Yano. As a junior scholar, I am also indebted to the more established scholars who took the time to critique and, more importantly, encourage the spirit of this project, including James Watson, Timothy Cheek, and Jeffrey Wasserstrom. I also thank Michael Schoenhals for his early review of the manuscript. Many thanks are also due to my editor, David Myers, at Rutgers University Press; his commitment to my project showed an admirable blend of cerebral insight and professional expediency.

As I learn the ropes of being a new assistant professor at Middle Tennessee State University, I am increasingly appreciative of my colleagues and students in the sociology and anthropology department who have given me an exceedingly comfortable and stimulating place to come to every day. I am especially grateful to the anthropology director, Kevin Smith, who gives special meaning to the word "mentor," and to my newfound friends and research partners, Jackie Eller, Celeste Ray, and Sarah Sherwood. John McDaniel has been particularly gracious in answering my stream of questions and requests, and our new chair, Ed Kick, has become a valued supporter.

I am equally beholden to my earliest mentors at Appalachian State University, particularly Patricia Beaver and Susan Keefe. As an undergraduate student at Appalachian, I learned that education is boundless. I also want to express special appreciation for Appalachian's China exchange program, and to its director, Marv Williamsen, for the unique venue through which I was introduced to the People's Republic. I am also privileged to acknowledge my Chinese colleagues and friends at Northeast University in Shenyang. Particular thanks also to Ma Hongnan and Li Xuemea for their research assistance.

I am deeply indebted to my parents, Walter and Marie Schrift, for their loving perseverance in raising and educating three daughters. Tani Schrift and Stacy Beneville represent the other two-thirds of my history and remind me of who I want to be. Many thanks also to the Pilkey family, particularly Orrin and Sharlene, for embracing me as one of their own. Finally, I thank my husband, Keith Pilkey, whose partnership through years of education, mobility, part-time jobs, babies, and Mao badges means everything to me at the end of the day.

Biography of
a Chairman
Mao Badge

Introduction

Mao Consumption
and the Chinese
Political Imaginary

During my second research excursion to the People's Republic of China in 1995, I lived in Beijing in order to explore public exhibitions of Mao's image in contemporary China. Early in the journey, with my husband and two-year-old son, I squeezed into one of Beijing's miniature taxicabs to travel to one of the many antique and curio markets that represent part of Beijing's economy. The driver asked the obligatory questions of what we were doing in China, and I explained that I was studying images of Mao Zedong. Amused, he broke into a boisterous song about his love for Chairman Mao, pounding his chest and laughing deliriously. Ever the ethnographer, I wanted to solicit information. How old was he during the Cultural Revolution? Had he always lived in Beijing? How did he come to drive a taxi? But he increased the volume and intensity of his rambunctious accolade of Chairman Mao, drowning out my questions. Fearful that he would surrender the steering wheel as well, I sat silent for the remainder of the trip. When we reached our destination, we tumbled out of the taxi; the driver, with utter calm and repose, took our money for the ride and politely asked if we would like him to return to pick us up. Before we left Beijing, we indeed had the pleasure of multiple transports with this melodious driver who continued his frenetic mockery of Chairman Mao. A former Red Guard, now in his mid-forties, he reflected on his Cultural Revolution experiences with a bittersweet drama that left the strong impression that Mao, in spirit if not in body (his crystal-encased corpse in Tiananmen aside), was, indeed, alive and well in contemporary China.

Mao's reappearance in the late twentieth century comes with a new look: Mao in pigtails; Mao on musical lighters blaring the "East is Red"; Mao's picture hanging from the walls of Beijing's affluent Cultural Revolution theme restaurants; and Mao badges displayed on shirts of university students. Mao's ambiguous and sometimes humorous revival in contemporary China leads us to ask: What does the perpetual iconographic presentation of Mao signify in the modern world? A handful of Western scholars have suggested that the Mao revival is but one index by which we can understand Chinese citizens' ambiguity in establishing national identities in post-Mao China (Barmé 1996; Benewick 1995, 1999; Dutton 1998; Friedman 1994; Schell 1994; Schram 1994).

Though I am equally intrigued by the immortality of Mao's image, I am not sure it is possible to understand the endurance of Mao as a cultural and national symbol in China without first considering more fundamental questions surrounding the legacy of Mao's image: How was Mao's image consumed historically, and what does this consumption reveal about Chinese political and cultural identity? Who was responsible for the production of Mao's image, and how was Mao's image proliferated on such a massive scale? How have the consumption rites surrounding Mao's image changed, and how can the historical consumption of Mao's image inform our understanding of Mao's contemporary revival?

This study probes these questions through analysis of the consumption of Mao badges, with primary focus on the early Cultural Revolution period (1966–1969), when citizens produced, circulated, and consumed Mao's image en masse. Though this work integrates varied representations of Mao's image, I focus primarily on Mao badges for several reasons. First and foremost, badges were the most prolific medium through which Mao's image (with visual and written text) has been trafficked in Chinese history (Barmé1996). In addition, badges were (and are) imbued with value as collectibles so that vast quantities of badges survived the post–Cultural Revolution destruction of propaganda items. Finally, within Western scholarship, analyses of Mao badges are minimal (Benewick 1995, 1999; B. Bishop 1996; Dutton 1998; Schrift and Pilkey 1996; White 1994). The fact that Western scholarship is only beginning to take heed of Mao badges as an academic phenomenon stands in striking contrast to both Chinese writings on Mao badges and to the wealth of Western scholarship on other Chinese propaganda forms, including opera, *dazibao* (big-character posters), and literature. Thus, there is good reason to pursue a scholarly inquiry of badges as unique icons.

Finally, as textual emblems that lived through the Cultural Revolution up to the present, Mao badges illustrate the ways in which material goods reflect and refract the political and cultural theater that embeds them. Mao badges are highly original witnesses to a landscape of characters that stake a claim in China's national voice, from the Cultural Revolution's Red Guards to more contemporary global entrepreneurs and tourists. In this sense, Kopytoff's (1992) concept of a biography of material goods is applicable.

In this study I attempt to provide a biography of Mao badges to illustrate the power of the material and symbolic consumption of goods in untangling the local histories and voices that paralleled and intersected—even subverted—China's centralized voice. Premised on the notion that a dialectical relationship exists between centralized propaganda and public consumption, this study examines the scope of propaganda strategies and the people's ability to mediate national forces through the consumption of Mao badges. Mao badges provided a way for people to define themselves and to internalize and negotiate a dogmatic nationalist ideology during the Cultural Revolution. The diversion of badges from state-inspired propagandistic agents allowed them expansion into other arenas of meaning, reflecting Appadurai's (1992) notion that material objects follow trajectories of meanings in their life cycles. Initially intended to symbolize the people's devotion to and support of Mao Zedong, badges adopted lives that vastly transcended and outlived the initial intentions of their creators.

The Art of Symbolic Communication

Symbol manipulation through alternative communication channels serves as a primary strategy for Chinese cultural change. Whether they are Chinese opera, big-character posters, blackboards, wall newspapers, street-corner shows, funerary rites, storytellers, comics, folk songs, short stories, study meetings, children's literature, or paintings, alternative venues of expression are inseparable from Communist history. Mao strategically used varied media forms to rally sympathy and mobilize the masses. In Godwin Chu's words:

The experience of China deserves special scrutiny because it is a case in which the resources of the state have been vigorously mobilized to propagate new cultural patterns. . . . Every conceivable communication channel in China has been employed to carry the new messages, the new societal goals, and the new revolutionary values to the Chinese masses. (G. Chu 1979:3)

Alternative communication channels were not born of Mao's communism but, according to Yu (1979), they were the essence of it. Saich traces the use of the Chinese Communist Party's (CCP's) symbolic capital back to Yenan, where Mao taught revolutionaries how to attain power through an "inversionary discourse community that constructed its own language of belief" (1990:257). Mao sought popular and familiar venues to incite revolution. Beginning in his Yenan days, he cleverly capitalized on Chinese tradition by perpetuating new ideas through old means, such as folk songs, big-character posters, and opera. By 1948, he had successfully instituted literacy classes, people's schools, people's blackboards, newspaper-reading groups, people's revolutionary rooms, and rural theater throughout China.

Borrowing from historical tactics of dissent such as the 1919 May Fourth Movement, Mao emphasized accessibility in communication. As early as 1927, he equated the use of simple slogans and pictures to sending peasants to a political school. During his prerevolutionary days in Yenan, Mao relied on the simplification of language to make his Communist philosophy and agenda accessible to large numbers of people. To rally broad-based support for the Communist revolution, Mao appealed to the illiterate peasantry through simple slogans, pictures, and speeches. Indeed, Mao's ingenuity with symbolic language and pictorials, aptly characterized by Jones (1994) as his "semiotic guerrilla warfare," contributed enormously to the fulfillment of his revolutionary agenda.

Indeed, the symbolic manipulation of unofficial media continues in contemporary China. Landsberger (1995), for example, analyzes Chinese poster art as a historical and contemporary medium that reflects political and social change. According to Landsberger, poster art mirrors transitions in the power structure of the CCP. For example, in the 1980s the visual authority of deceased leaders Mao Zedong and Zhou Enlai was diluted with proliferation of Deng Xiaoping images.

With Mao's influence, communication changed in style and content. Media that were historically sponsored by the people transformed into centrally authored and disseminated propaganda. Mao formalized propaganda, expediting forms to reflect official policy rather than popular opinion (G. Chu 1978). Media content transformed from being slow and spontaneous to a more uniform template of revolutionary heroism.

Mao's aptitude with unofficial media was, in part, a matter of practicality: he did not have access to means of mass communication. Alternative media enabled him to bypass the official media over which he had limited control before 1949. Such nontraditional avenues of communication offered Mao a forum that was highly public, interesting, interactive, and familiar. The genius of Communist propaganda lies not only with the dissemination of political agendas through creative channels, but with the ways in which those channels demand active participation, thereby manufacturing an illusion of consent. The participatory nature of Communist propaganda, on one level, provided Mao with an appearance of consensus necessary to manufacture consent for revolutionary change (Chu and Chin 1978; Leijonhufvud 1990; Pye 1979). Robert Bishop (1989), for example, states that Mao realized his goal to use media to propagate policies, educate, organize, and mobilize the masses through China's one dependable and abundant resource—the masses.

Overwrought distinctions between official and popular culture unduly dichotomize and obscure the nuances of symbolic exchange. One would be hard pressed to find a better illustration of the tenuous nature of such divisions than Chinese popular culture, in which popular expression involves appropriation of centralized propaganda as much as grassroots creations. The participatory nature of Communist propaganda accommodates the inevitable dilution of state-initiated narratives. Hong (1979), for example, discusses the backlash of the Maoist strategy of symbol manipulation in the context of the Chinese public's initiative in using symbols according to their own interests. Similarly, Wu (1991) assigns being Chinese to the process of amalgamating, restructuring, reinventing, and reinterpreting oneself via symbols. The use of communication as a means to change is not unique to Chinese culture, of course; however, the myriad forms through which communication is effected in this culture invite possibilities of a dialectical arena of expression that is unparalleled.

Such studies on the shadows of political culture offer a refreshing corrective to scholarship on China that is too often weighted by a preoccupation with cultural identity as a hegemonic drama passively received by a naive and impressionable entourage. While it would be neglectful to rob China of its dizzying political dogma, it would be equally careless to dismiss the semiotic possibilities of that dogma.

The Language of Badges

The replication of Mao himself as a mass-produced "iconic vehicle" (Aijmer 1996) during the Cultural Revolution was unprecedented; curiously, Mao had become one of the venues he had relied on to propagate the revolution. Though scholars stress that Chinese Communist propaganda relies on every imaginable unofficial medium available to the public, Mao badges are conspicuously absent in discussions of alternative communication media. Godwin Chu (1979) acknowledges the accessibility of big-character posters to the general public, because they required only brush, ink, and paper. While Chu doesn't mention the additional requirement of literacy, others emphasize the difficulties of using traditional print media throughout Chinese Communist history due to large-scale illiteracy. Robert Bishop (1989), for example, comments on the useless nature of printed media for illiterate peasants. Berger (1997) describes, at length, the relationship between illiteracy and the popularity of *Mao's Quotations,* also known as the Little Red Book. According to Berger, the Little Red Book was particularly appealing to the people due to the short and simple nature of the quotations. In fact, though almost every Chinese person owned the book, many were unable to read; hence, the government organized study groups aimed at teaching illiterate members of society quotations by memorization.

As visual texts featuring the most basic, if any, text, early Mao badges transcended vast differences in literacy and education levels and provided a sense of familiarity by invoking traditional cultural symbols. Badges successfully diluted a state-inspired narrative predicated on a feverish iconoclasm and grassroots rebellion. As emblems that were worn, badges also wielded a dual weight, their adornment suggesting an appearance of unanimity with that narrative.

In addition to informing the masses of the correct political line to be followed during the Cultural Revolution, badges offered the illusion of conformity to political dictum because individuals wore these badges, which was interpreted as one's political expression. As emblems displayed on one's clothes, Mao badges effortlessly created the appearance of enthusiasm and engagement. They were an especially powerful medium because of their accessibility; they were portable and immediately visible testaments of devotion to Mao. The badges also transcended the monotony of obligatory study groups and meetings by featuring esthetically appealing images, thereby inviting even more enthusiastic participation. As Landsberger has pointed out, "No amount of communal study or newspaper reading ever could have the same effect as the direct experience of being confronted with striking visual propaganda" (1996:197). Landsberger also proves this point well in a study of Communist posters in which bold and daring images immediately engage in ways that text cannot.

Mao badges were especially potent in accommodating cultural change by virtue of the intertextuality they offered. Hwang (1978) discusses the advantages of certain propaganda forms for the hybridity that he defines as the combination of pictorials and text. Mao badges combined a rich visual and written text with a multitude of meaningful esthetic stimuli through their imagery, text, color, shape, size, and material components. As material and symbolic collages, badges embodied a wealth of esthetic resources through which even the most subtle semiotic conflation was possible. Mao badges stimulated visually and emotionally, infusing state-sponsored narratives with a polysemy that subverted unidirectional consumption.

Consumption

Consumption is a uniquely dynamic interchange between humans and their symbolic and material worlds that negotiates historical memory, individual agency, and larger political and economic agendas. (For the most comprehensive general discussions of consumption, see Appadurai 1992; Douglas and Isherwood 1989; McCracken 1988; and Miller 1987.)

Recent approaches to consumption resist the reduction of goods to the intentions of their producers. Miller (1987) aptly characterizes the process by which an object transcends its primary intent as recontextualization, placing equal merit on both the production and reception of material culture. Other perspectives focus on the social uses of consumption to assign status, and pursue or resist state-directed agendas in relation to the construction of cultural and national identities.

Research on status attainment and consumption focuses on creations of value and acts of display. In one of the earliest attempts to understand social roles via consumption choices, Simmel (1904) argued that with the advent of the Industrial Revolution, the conceptual dynamic of fashion emerged as the lower classes pursued social mobility by imitating the material world of the elite. With the onslaught of the mass production of goods, the upper classes could no longer maintain their distinctive status through the patina of goods obtained through classic inheritance.

The wonderfully rich concept of patina refers to the symbolic properties of goods, the "invisible ink" (McCracken 1988) of authenticity guarded by the upper classes. This might relate, for example, to signs of wear that accumulate on an object from generations of ownership. Another illustration rests with the subtle nuances with which one handles, displays, or speaks about goods. Williams (1982) provides lively examples of such sumptuary rules among the French aristocracy, pointing to Marie Antoinette's distinctive taste for simplicity in the face of the "vulgar" display of the salons of the nouveaux riches. Schooled in such distinctions, nobility easily identified what McCracken

(1988) terms "status counterfeiters," as in the example Williams (1982) provides of the aristocrat who visited the home of a woman whose arrangement of goods insulted his class-based sensibilities: he knew, upon entering, that he would never be able to make love to her.

The emergence of industrialization destabilized the sumptuary insulation of the privileged classes. Novelty replaced patina as a signifier of status as the marketplace lured elite classes to distinguish themselves through the luxuries of accumulation and expendability. The realm of novelty, however, offered cheap substitution in the face of mass production; as McCracken (1988) notes, an object cannot exist in infinite quantity and be rare at the same time. According to Simmel (1904), with mass production the lower classes easily accessed the material accouterments of the elite. This "trickle-down" process drove production to unimaginable heights.

McCracken (1988) modifies Simmel's trickle-down theory by suggesting that a more nuanced "flight and chase" dynamic served as the culprit of production. McCracken (1988) argues that the desire among the upper classes to differentiate themselves from cheap imitators is what powered production. As commoners appropriated material goods, the elite sought ever more inventive avenues to distinguish themselves.

While McCracken (1988) offers a particularly thorough general theory of consumption, other scholars have also pioneered thoughtful meditations on the relationship between consumption and social roles. Douglas and Isherwood's (1989) classic work on the meanings of goods offers a more in-depth assessment of the cultural aspects of consumption, while Appadurai (1992) provides a timeless collection of varied cultural meanings of material objects. Weiner and Schneider's (1989) collection of essays on cloth also stands out as a rich illustration of material goods to forge and legitimate gendered and class identities. Similarly, Mintz (1985) tackles a pervasive material product—sugar—to explicate the relationships between goods and social identities and roles. These classics invigorated anthropological scholarship by attending to the oft-ignored realm of consumption in the economic life cycles of cultures. By initiating an anthropology of consumption, these works encouraged an ever-more sophisticated scholarship that integrates consumption, nationalism, and the global trade in goods to relate to specific ethnographic settings (Howes 1996; Jarman 1997; Miller 1998; Orlove 1997).

The cultural and political context of the Chinese Cultural Revolution is a far cry from Western aristocracy, however. The enduring theoretical tenets of these historical works offer a rich premise for analysis of Mao badges in several ways. As objects that involved mass production and consumption, badges dictated and reflected social roles and identities during the revolution. As a transnational phenomenon in the contemporary public landscape of tourist markets, political protests, and museum displays of cultural heritage, badge consumption continues to elucidate cultural and national identities.

Theoretical discussions of consumption have taken on new dimensions as scholars address consumption practices in the modern global world. At the forefront of globalization studies is the premise that the flow of cultural goods in the world today cannot be fully understood without reference to the cultural, political, and economic transactions among nations that result in the weakening of national and cultural boundaries and potential blurring of identities (Kearney 1995). Premised on the pioneering notion that both nation and tradition are malleable abstractions rather than superorganic entities (Anderson 1983; Hobsbawm and

Ranger 1983), current scholarship tends to reinvent tradition without lamenting cultural change as a trend toward
global homogeneity.

A skillful example of such work relating to China can
be found in Watson's (1998) collection of essays on the lo-
calization, or Asianization, of the fast-food conglomerate
McDonald's. Similarly, Evans and Donald (1999) forcefully
argue for a dialogic interpretation of popular culture, all the
more refreshing in a collection of commentaries on Communist propaganda posters. The very nature of Barmé's
(1999) work on dissident culture suggests individual agency
in contrast to official culture. However, Barmé's relentless
cynicism regarding "nonofficial" culture cautions against
simplistic categories. The very use of his adoption of "nonofficial" instead of the more popular "unofficial" is based
on his premise that even "dissident" culture in China must
be understood in relation to official agendas. At the same
time, Barmé excuses himself from engaging larger debates
related to globalization.

Dutton's (1998) stream-of-consciousness amalgamation
of tales of "street-life" China offers a finely nuanced, if occasionally elusive, vision of unofficial culture, including a
healthy section on Mao iconography based primarily on
Zhou's work (1993). Dutton's stylistic meanderings resist a
sustained argument throughout the scenes he describes. Although it is enjoyable to read, his approach inevitably frus-
trates, particularly in light of his pessimistic finale on the
one-dimensionality of contemporary consumerism, illustrated by his questionable interpretation of the robotic sense
of Chinese fashion.

The repositioning of indigenous groups as being
complicitous in modernization projects rather than passively
accepting them offers a welcome alternative to myopic views
of cultural change as necessarily a product of hegemonic

interests. A refreshing analytical utility results, redirecting anthropologists to the multidimensional nature of cultural change; Westernization is no longer presented as a tsunami of change. However, scholarship on globalization tends to downplay the dynamic nature of premodern, non-Western traditions in favor of elaborations on modern hybrid concoctions of heritage. Too often, invented traditions take priority as the only, or most interesting, ones and obscure their historical legacies. It is as if only when indigenous cultures are confronted with the megaliths of McDonalds and Western media that they find the creativity to play with, or hybridize, tradition.

In this study I depart from the proclivity to privilege global modernity in the invention of tradition by proposing that tradition has long been a dynamic and syncretic—or playful—manifestation of identity. This is not to suggest that the new inventions of Mao reflect a jazzed-up version of the historical Mao. Clearly, processes of cultural change spawn uniquely syncretized transnational public exchanges in China, resulting in a plethora of Maos. However, it is only through consideration of the genealogy of Mao's image that we can appreciate the dynamic nature of Chinese tradition. The nuances of traditional Mao consumption present a necessary starting point for a more comprehensive debate on the proposed novelties of Mao's revival in the global age.

Wasserstrom and Perry's (1994) approach to political theater offers an admirable standard for analysis of Chinese popular and political expression as performative yet historically grounded. In analyses of the 1989 movement, contributors describe the various actors and stylistic devices as innovations upon cultural traditions of dissent. Perry (1994), for example, describes the efficacy with which protestors borrowed from historical traditions of remonstrance, including the emphasis on petitions, banners, and dialogue with leaders. Wasserstrom (1991) contrasts the 1989 movement with symbolic expressions in both the Cultural Revolution and the May Fourth movement. For example, he explores the goddess of democracy as a syncretic vehicle that draws upon Western ideals as well as Chinese folk religious traditions and socialist realist techniques. In a similar vein, Esherick and Wasserstrom (1994) tease out Cultural Revolution legacies in the 1989 movement, including the use of wall posters, free travel to Beijing, and the presentation of Mao's portrait. The authors also describe contrasts between the movements, pointing to the absence of anti-Western rhetoric and the noncommittal references to party leaders.

Christmas with Chinese Characteristics: The Ethnographic Setting

I first visited China during the 1990–1991 academic year as a student of anthropology and as an English teacher, with my husband, Keith. Much of my preliminary reading centered on the 1949 revolution, Mao Zedong, and the Cultural Revolution. I also read a great deal about changes in gender roles and family life following China's economic reform policies. Intrigued by the vibrant atmosphere of cultural change taking place for women, I went to China with the intention of doing research on Chinese gender issues.

Our Chinese hosts housed Keith and me in a hotel allotted for foreign guests, or, more accurately, for Western guests. The rooms resembled those of a Western hotel, fully equipped with modern bathrooms, carpeting, television, and telephone. We were privileged this way because we were English teachers. To my dismay, the housing for foreign students was conspicuously different, and at first I was disappointed by the housing arrangements, having anticipated a year of roughing it like a "true" anthropologist. As it turned out, our housing was quirky enough, and my idealism waned as I came to appreciate amenities like a private western toilet and freedom from the cockroaches that inhabited the foreign residence hall.

The Chinese categorized all Westerners as foreign exchange English teachers, including a neighboring missionary family. The details of our daily lives with our missionary neighbors annoyed me, particularly when they entertained droves of Chinese students and cheered their success in converting them to Christianity. A few months into our stay, they proudly proclaimed that their work had been so successful that they had run out of Bibles and had to smuggle a new shipment into the country. I silently wondered why the students were so drawn to these missionaries. Were these Chinese really interested in converting to Christianity? Their interest appeared to be in sharp contrast to my first day in the classroom, when my own students asked if I was a missionary. When I said no, they all cheered. Why, then, were so many young Chinese parading through my neighbors' room? I thought my questions were answered one day when a Chinese friend stopped by after a prolonged stay with the missionaries.

"Did you enjoy your visit?" I pressed.

"Oh, yes," my friend answered, then proceeded to talk about the virtues of studying English via the Bible. Of course! The Chinese students were not interested at all in conversion to Christianity; they were "English Christians." I was reminded of a story that had hallmarked missionaries in my mind ever since I had heard it. Offended by nudity among natives in the Pacific, missionaries had proceeded to introduce clothing. The natives, offended by the constraints of the clothing, cut strategic holes in the clothing to free their genitals.

I felt at once smug and comfortable until my friend,

still smiling, told me that he had heard of my interest in the Cultural Revolution. Would I be interested in hearing his own story? My immediate reaction was positive, but then I paused. He was in his early twenties, which would have made him a newborn when the Cultural Revolution began. How much of a story could he have? The natives who had cut holes in their missionary clothes turned into the lampooned natives screaming, "Hide the TV! The anthropologists are coming!" I watched my friend leave my room and imagined a young Chinese man with hidden Bible, perforated clothes, a hidden television, and dreams of speaking English and visiting America.

My growing interest in Cultural Revolution memorabilia struck our Chinese friends and students as odd and as being far removed from the promises of economic reform. At the time, Mao's iconic revival was merely a twinkle in the eye of a rapidly changing nation, particularly in the industrial pocket of Shenyang. When I got to China, I knew little of Mao badges or other Cultural Revolution iconography, except for stories about my father-in-law's travels to China in the early 1980s, and a fellow Western exchange student's modest collection of Mao badges. But Keith's intrigue with Communist propaganda, as well as our penchant for discovering the underbelly of the city, led us to weekend explorations of street markets. Living in Shenyang, an industrial city that offers little esthetic appeal for foreign visitors, we accessed a unique inroad to the Mao badge market. In 1990, Shenyang vendors did not market Mao badges as they do now; indeed, we came across badges rather accidentally.

During one of our first visits to the market, we discovered a handkerchief full of badges inconspicuously poking out; we pulled out the handkerchief and bought the ten or so badges inside. The badges struck me as unspectacular, but they encouraged Keith to explore more aggressively, asking vendors for them specifically. These vendors, typically middle-aged men, were at first frustrated by our lack of enthusiasm for the real antiques they wanted to sell. As we persisted, the response grew; within weeks, similar handkerchiefs and boxes of badges appeared. Upon seeing us coming, vendors summoned us to show us their badges. The diversity of badge themes caught my interest, and I informally sought interpretations from any vendor or friend willing to explain. Enthralled by the infinite variety and meanings of badge themes, I became a closet enthusiast and joined Keith in his effort to seek, interpret, and collect these items. The response from vendors grew exponentially. As we became better versed in the meanings of badges, vendors brought more elaborate ones to the market. On many occasions, while trying to explain the vastness and significance of Cultural Revolution badges, they asked us to watch their stations for them while they hopped on their bicycles to bring more badges back. Keith and I acquired hundreds of badges this way for approximately twenty dollars.

My interest in badges heightened as I became more confident with the dynamics of the informal markets. Haggling over money was an integral element of any street market exchange, and Westerners were considered foolish for not doing so. The verbal exchange more often than not led to unexpected insights. In one exchange, for example, a vendor rationalized his exorbitant prices for Mao memorabilia by shouting, "You don't understand, China's Saddam!" while pointing to Mao's image.

One morning, I arrived at a market quite early in the hope of obtaining a promised ceramic statue of Mao and Lin Biao. When I arrived, the vendor bicycled home to pick it up. He returned, asking for too much money. I resisted, realizing that the time I was spending in negotiating the

Lin Biao statue that morning would be the first stage of a longer exchange. This was a particularly difficult situation, because I really wanted that statue. But I had also developed a rapport with the vendors in this particular market. I had gained respectability as a haggling woman who curbed her husband's unthriftiness by refusing any amount he appeared eager to pay. Our good cop/bad cop routine provided grand theater for all of us and often led to laughter—and prices that were radically lowered for us though still comically high for the vendors. The transactions usually ended with my grudging nod of consent and shared sympathies between Keith and the vendors on the nature of love, marriage, and women.

Confronted with Lin Biao and the vagaries of desire, I remained unwilling to sacrifice my haggling gains. After a prolonged exchange, I sighed and shook my head. The vendor tucked the statue into his coat and walked away. The process would continue the next day, we both knew, and I was anxious to get back to my room to thaw my frozen toes. As we waved our good-byes, the vendor sauntered down the street, whereupon a tall man, covered in coat and scarves from head to toe, approached him from a side street. After a brief exchange, he handed the vendor a pile of bills, took the statue, and left. Intrigued and dismayed, I asked the vendor about the incident for days afterwards. He acted as surprised as I was, or at least he was not forthcoming. As consolation—and no doubt motivated by further profits—he obtained a similar statue from someone among his friends and presented it to me. However, on this one Mao stood solo, with only a visible light gray outline where Lin Bao had been. I bought the piece out of a sense of obligation but mourned the fish that got away for years afterward. Today, the statue is as an anomaly among the many reproductions that have swamped the antique market, and it serves as a compelling reminder of the glories and pitfalls of my desire. Vendors also referred us to local badge collectors who displayed for us some of the most spectacular badges I have ever seen. A fellow Westerner and stamp collector, Bob White, became a fellow badge collector The acuity he had applied to stamp iconography had impressed me long before we came to China, and now, accompanied by him, we delved into an even deeper layer of street market memorabilia. One collector invited Keith and Bob to his home to show them a collection of approximately one hundred three-dimensional, multicolored badges. After some bargaining, they bought the whole collection for several hundred dollars. We then laid the collection on Bob's living-room floor and, over several hours, divided it up, taking turns choosing the badges we wanted. It was a memorable evening, expressing the depths we had reached as collectors. Splayed across the floor among the badges until the wee hours, we chose with the intensity and strategy of a chess game. This purchase signaled the end of our intensive collecting efforts. We had spent several hundred dollars on a collection of over one thousand badges, exhausting our meager disposable income.

From the beginning, I was excited by the idea of researching badges but was bound by multiple inhibitions. Despite my intrigue with badges, I had qualms about collecting them, which were magnified by my growing interest in studying them. In retrospect, it is clear that my inhibitions were related to my naiveté as a beginning anthropologist. I had seen many interesting native items decorating anthropology professors' homes, but anthropologists are conspicuously quiet about the thrill of exotic acquisitions in the cultures they study. It remains an unspoken notion that material consumption in other cultures equals slumming with the tourists. How, then, could I possibly justify scholarly research on something that my husband and I had collected, paid money for, had even cultivated our own corner market on? It seemed an impossible sacrilege to elevate my material consumption to the standards of anthropological research. Still, I quietly pursued my interest in these badges, working on translations and conducting interviews centered on Cultural Revolution experiences.

The growing ethic of consumption in China further compounded my ambivalence. Having embraced a decade of economic reforms, urban Chinese embraced free market enterprises and Western culture. As English-speaking Westerners, we attracted an overwhelming amount of attention. Strangers approached us on the streets to implore us to provide private English lessons, announcing the time and place we were to meet. Having been insulated from other cultures for the long period of the Cultural Revolution, our Chinese friends were hungry for cultural interchanges and delighted in Western music, dance, and customs.

Besides his good looks and his ability to share in housework, Keith was lauded for his good sense of humor. If I was shy about the dual ambiguities of performing my own cultural heritage while commodifying China's, Keith's playful intrigue with the theater of modernity overshadowed my reservations. He regularly wore badges in public to the delight of our Chinese friends. He was happy to display our collection of badges to our visitors. When we attended a local concert of the rock musician Cui Jian, it was Keith who first rose to dance in the aisles beside the uniformed guards who monitored the concert. The crowd of avant-garde youth followed his lead, circling Keith as he performed his spastic, hard-core-influenced Chinese disco (he regained his senses after one student suggested they throw bottles at the stage). Keith taught students lyrics to Carpenter songs (a local favorite), singing with abandon; he sent away for John

Denver tapes and, upon request, imitated Michael Jackson.

Our Chinese friends quickly realized that something of a physical comedian was in their midst after Keith gave a stunning, animated lecture for the university's English Club. This club was an umbrella group at the university that hosted lectures and weekly "free talks," or English corners, where Chinese students solicited native English speakers for conversational exchanges. Transforming his slide-projector blunders into a slapstick routine during an English Club lecture, Keith finished to the roaring applause of two hundred.

Word spread quickly, and a consensus was soon reached: Keith would be the Santa Claus for the English Club's Christmas show. While the missionaries seemed thrilled to shape the biggest rendition of Christmas in a city of eight million, Keith anguished over his new role. I began to work with Chinese friends on his outfit. Students collected cotton rations to provide the fluff that we attached to Keith's red long johns. As Christmas approached, it became clear that the obligation to "perform" Christmas in China would not be Keith's alone. Christmas parties surfaced everywhere, and foreign presence was in demand. We accepted early invitations with gratitude; however, as we began to attend parties, we tired of the pressure to do Christmas, or, more broadly, to do America.

The evening of the English Club Christmas show arrived during a wintry blizzard to hundreds of excited Chinese students; a poised, edgy missionary family; a worn-out, once funny Santa Claus; and a handful of jaded Americans. The students directed Keith to go to the auditorium early and wait backstage. They escorted me to the auditorium, and I took my seat. As time passed, the Chinese host worried that Keith had not yet shown up. Fearing that he may have gotten lost in the snow, she recruited me to walk back through the blizzard to find him. We walked quite a way, arm-in-arm, calling Keith's name—to no avail. My friend was becoming frantic, fearing the collapse of the evening for which she had worked so hard. I assured her that Keith had a very good sense of direction, but she did not respond. Feeling a little hopeless myself, I jokingly suggested that we call Keith by his real name. My friend spiritedly responded, calling through the hiss of the blizzard, "Santa Claus, where are you?" I joined her: "Santa Claus! Santa Claus! Please come home!" We were soon loudly pleading with Santa to answer, admonishing the reindeer for losing their way, and laughing deliriously. We then fell into a snow bank. With numb toes and tangled arms, we turned away from the whimsical fantasy we were enjoying and returned to the auditorium. We arrived at the auditorium to find the missionaries perturbed, the audience eager, and a smiling, frostbitten Santa Claus, icicles clinging to his cotton-trimmed beard, with his crowning glory—an army-green Mao cap. The Chinese host gathered herself together and strode on stage, introducing the first performer of the night: a popular male Chinese singer whose version of John Denver's "Country Roads" had the young women in the audience swooning. I sat through the show exhausted by the painful disequilibrium of doing Christmas in China. I was homesick and bothered by the skinny, wet Mao-draped Santa Claus ludicry called Christmas in China. I wanted to leave and be anywhere but in that auditorium. Instead, I joined the other Americans on stage and limped through another rendition of "Jingle Bells."

Issues of cultural appropriation are integral to understanding the context of Mao consumption. Larger issues of culture theft that implicate and extend well beyond me were (and are) ever present in my mind. The height of my anxieties occurred when we left China. We considered the possibility that we would be relieved of our badge collection by Chinese customs officials. We packed the badges in our clothes and hoped for the best. When we went through customs, we were, in fact, delayed for suspicious material in our luggage. Officials searched our bag and pulled out a Cultural Revolution alarm clock that had flagged the X-ray monitor as a ticking device. The officials grinned at the ticking clock, its hands the waving arms of Red Guards, and tossed it back into the bag.

My own self-imposed yokes of propriety inhibited my ethnographic approach to some degree. I had been doing rich ethnographic work on gender and family issues, and my ethnography on badges was comparatively meager. The sphere of family and gender encouraged an exchange of information, providing ample opportunity for respondents to inquire about Western culture and customs. There was no ready Western equivalent for Mao badges and the Cultural Revolution. Respondents were more interested in changing conversations about the Cultural Revolution to the preferred topic of economic reform. Many dismissed the Cultural Revolution as an era of madness, discussing their lives during the time with both humor and bitterness.

My ambivalence also raised questions that are fundamental to the anthropological process as we engage the transnational world. Anthropology's strength has always been its voluntary reflexivity and willingness to reinvent itself. The poetic and critical call and response between product and process that marks anthropology lends an integrity that is the life-blood of the discipline.

In hindsight, 1990 was a remarkable time to be in the People's Republic. Well into the throes of economic reform yet fresh out of the pro-democracy movement, China was on the brink of the many cultural changes that were much more grounded when I returned for continued research in

1995. My memory of Christmas in China strikes me as poetic metaphor for the elusive cacophony of what Appadurai describes as "ethnoscapes." As an anthropology student, I was well versed in the staple of culture shock. Yet, I was not prepared for the syncretic modernity that framed my own culture shock when I lived in China. At that point, I had not been exposed to the emergent literature on transnationalism and hybrid traditions. I just felt like a bad anthropologist ensnared in what I perceived to be a distorted version of my own culture.

A few years later, on the 1993 centenary of Mao's birthday, Chinese collectors and scholars began to publish texts on Mao badges. I returned to China in 1995, obtained numerous texts on Mao badges, and worked, with assistance, on complete translations. I also conducted further interviews with badge collectors and gathered an extensive array of archival materials on Chinese popular and political culture. By 1995 the topic of Mao iconography was more visible. Mao icons swamped the tourist markets and had assumed rich and varied positions in Chinese culture following the 1993 Mao rebirth.

The study of Mao propaganda in contemporary China can be politically tricky. The very nature of the premise of my work—that Mao propaganda is rife with symbolic meaning—was also tricky, as these symbolic meanings continue to be manipulated by the Chinese people and the government alike. The meltdown of suspicion surrounding social science research in the People's Republic of China facilitated my field research, however, and I benefited from the leniency of the Chinese institutions that supported my wish to conduct research in China as an exchange scholar—without babysitting the details of my research project.

Resources and Methods

Few undertakings in contemporary academia match the novelty of conducting research on Mao badges. While a great deal of attention has been paid to various forms of Chinese propaganda, an extensive, systematic study of Mao badges has been nonexistent in the Western world. In fact, Mao badges are barely mentioned in discussions of the *Maore* (Mao craze). This has been less an issue of academic ingenuity than of timing. Mao badges have only recently resurfaced as China is entering an era where the fallout of the Cultural Revolution can be more widely heard.

Since the centenary of Mao's birth in 1993, Chinese scholars have produced a wealth of material focused solely on Mao badges. Catalogues featuring private collections of badges have been published, badge research associations have been established, and at least two texts on Mao badges have been written.

My approach to field research on political propaganda reflects methods employed by other scholars of Chinese popular and political thought. I gathered data in formal ways, conducting structured interviews with Chinese citizens and Mao collectors. Scholars estimate that over two billion Mao badges were created during the Chinese Cultural Revolution. The Chinese Communist Party's recall of badges during the later years of the Cultural Revolution, as well as the destruction of badges by individuals after the Cultural Revolution, have reduced the number of badges that exist today. However, as I will discuss in chapter 4, the badge recall did not necessarily result in their mass destruction. Collectors often salvaged badges at recycling centers; defying instructions to turn the badges in, individuals have stowed away badges until the present day. Estimates on the total number of Cultural Revolution badges that exist today are not available; however, the individuals who have publicized their collections claim they number in the tens to hundreds of thousands. Chinese collectors typically report owning hundreds of badges.

In the process of doing this research, I saw tens of thousands of badges. After preliminary interviews about badges, I chose approximately two thousand of them for more in-depth interviews. These badges came from my own collection, those catalogued by Chinese collectors, and those of my respondents. Key respondents included a variety of badge and propaganda collectors and former Red Guards. They ranged in age from the early forties to the late sixties. While respondents easily answered questions about specific badges and generally recalled their Cultural Revolution experiences, it was difficult to elicit specific information about actual trades that took place twenty years earlier. Often, respondents answered questions about Mao icons and loyalty to Mao with a performance, teaching me how to do the loyalty dances that citizens performed every morning during the Cultural Revolution, as well as by teaching me Cultural Revolution songs.

I weighted my interviews toward what I perceived as the most tangible aspect of my project: interpretations of the badges themselves. These interviews reflected an extensive and in-depth knowledge of the expansive symbolic meanings of Mao's image, providing a solid foundation for my discussion of normative and anomalous themes (chapter 2) as well as providing me with a wealth of examples of badges discussed throughout this work. I also relied on the informalities of participant-observation, proceeding with my research in ways reminiscent of Gold's discussion of "guerrilla interviewing" in urban China, defined as "unchaperoned, spontaneous but structured participant observation and interviews as opportunities present themselves" (1989:180). Myriad examples of this technique occurred in my own research: jumping out of a taxi to chase down a young female student in Beijing who was sporting a small Mao badge on her shirt; dining in Cultural Revolution theme restaurants for hours at a time in Beijing; trying to explain the very odd request for a copy of a menu in those same restaurants to the restaurant manager; collecting Cultural Revolution periodicals that were being thrown away; and visiting Mao's mausoleum in Beijing.

In many ways, this project was not a traditional field project. I chose to supplement my fieldwork with archival research at home, reviewing Chinese periodicals and texts from the Cultural Revolution that were often unavailable in China. Following other scholars of political and popular culture in China, I developed research on Mao badges with significant reliance on primary source material. During the summer of 1995, I conducted extensive archival research, visiting China collections at Harvard University, the University of Pennsylvania, Yale University, the Library of Congress, and the University of Washington. Asian Studies collections in the United States were particularly helpful given the destruction of primary resources in China following the Cultural Revolution. From China archives I collected hundreds of primary source materials, including premier weeklies published during the Cultural Revolution, Red Guard publications, and firsthand accounts of the revolution. Materials published during the revolution are, of course, heavily politicized. However, I use this material to convey the politicization that was the very fabric of Chinese culture during the Cultural Revolution.

My archival approach was also greatly enhanced by the current proliferation of memoirs written about the Cultural Revolution and published outside of China. Contextualized primarily in the experiences of intellectuals and Red Guards during the Chinese Cultural Revolution, these Chinese voices from the "lost generation" are particularly valuable as they skew the image of a homogeneous population during the Cultural Revolution. Unfettered by contemporary politics in the People's Republic, these versions entail an autonomous rendering of events during the Cultural Revolution that is difficult to replicate in interviews in-country.

These versions do not refute that a centralized authoritarianism was violently distributed during the Cultural Revolution, yet they reveal fragile crevices of individual expression that were, and continue to be, created and employed by the Chinese people.

My research reflects more of a cultural studies approach than I had first intended. However, I now feel such an approach suits a study of badges well. I am not convinced that a different approach would have been possible or more productive; perhaps that remains to be seen. Certainly, the tried and true ethnographic method takes a beating with ethnohistorical work, though issues of historical memory in relation to retellings of badge exchange and consumption would offer valuable insight. It is telling, however, that most research on Chinese material and popular culture, particularly the recent attempts to theorize badges, privileges textual analyses.

I am particularly grateful for the resources provided by two Chinese scholars of Mao badges in doing this project, Zhou Jihou and Li Xuemei, both of whom are authors of the only two existing texts on Mao badges. Both authors welcomed my interest in conducting research on Mao badges and provided me with a copy of their texts and with their insights. Zhou Jihou, a long-time collector in Guizhou, has written the longest text on badges, based on his own research, collection, and communication with other collectors (Zhou 1993). Though Zhou is an avid badge collector, he attempts a scholarly approach to his study, focusing more on badge history, symbolism, and distribution than collecting activities. Disturbed by what he characterizes as the superficial nature of collecting badges for profit in China today, Zhou earnestly promotes the research of badges. Li, who has a Ph.D. in political science, focuses her research on the nature of collecting in China, providing a somewhat more academic text that details badge history, symbolism, and consumption (Li 1993). Both texts, published in Chinese, reflect the difficulties of doing work on Mao propaganda in China. Both are primarily descriptive, without any lengthy critical analyses of the political implications of badges, and, particularly with Zhou, often couched in praise of the Communist regime. The 1993 publication of both texts was timely, taking advantage of Mao's centenary. Both authors produced highly informative texts that have been invaluable in my own research.

Chapter Overview

This study begins with an overview of the Cultural Revolution in chapter 1. It was during the early years of the Cultural Revolution that Mao, the heroic—and mortal—revolutionary leader, was transformed into Mao the icon. This introductory chapter addresses the conversion as a result of a legacy of propaganda that manufactured consent at the very same time that it manufactured Mao, and by the profitable consumption strategies that used Mao to establish politically expedient public identities. Though subsequent discussions of badge content and circulation are contextualized to specific Cultural Revolution movements when appropriate, the aim of this chapter is to provide a basic historical context for the generalist. Chapter 2 outlines the manufacture of Mao badges from the Communist party's Yenan days through the Cultural Revolution. This chapter also addresses the content of pre–Cultural Revolution badges, as well as the eventual recall of badges, first in 1969, then again following Mao's death.

A comprehensive examination of badge themes during the Cultural Revolution follows in chapter 3. With a range of representative badges, this chapter covers normative badge themes, including both pictorial images and written slogans. It then moves into a discussion of anomalous badges, debating the validity of decentralization and popular expression in the production of badges.

Chapters 4 and 5 examine badges in relation to their exchange and consumption during the Cultural Revolution. Chapter 4 discusses the relation of badges to correct political etiquette or customary codes of behavior during the Cultural Revolution. Badge exchange and display are cast in relationship to the establishment, maintenance, and the appropriation of political virtue, first among Red Guards and then among the population as a whole. Closely linked is the argument in chapter 5 that the constant and appropriate consumption of Mao's image vis-à-vis badges shielded political impropriety and accommodated Chinese conceptualizations of reciprocity. To illustrate this point I discuss the use of Mao propaganda as ritual gifts, fashion statements, and conduits to study English.

Chapters 4 and 5 propose that the very nature of Mao badges as unambiguous symbols of devotion to Mao is the essence of their ability to simultaneously wallow in and veer away from official dogma. The result is a shift in focus to the historical congruities in the manifestation of Chinese cultural identity vis-à-vis indigenous conceptualization of ritual form, and the proper maintenance of social relationships based on the time-worn but variegated ethic of Chinese reciprocity. The underlying argument resists simplistic interpretations of a Maoist personality cult by

suggesting the integrity of indigenous conceptual categories in the face of massive culture change.

Chapter 6 focuses on the reemergence of Cultural Revolution relics in contemporary China to address ways in
which popular and official historical reenactments of Mao
intersect with globalization processes. The varied ironic and
ambiguous manifestations of Mao in the forms of good-luck
charms, political symbols, Cultural Revolution theme restaurants, and Mao badge markets and museums reveal a
performative and cathartic interaction with history. The re-
ritualization of Mao's image also suggests a playful and critical engagement of a transnational future.

1

Badges in

Context

The Early Years of the Cultural Revolution

Mao's flawed socioeconomic initiatives in the 1950s, including the Hundred Flowers campaign in 1957 and the Great Leap Forward in 1958, tainted his image of revolutionary heroism. Having positioned China on the edge of financial and social bankruptcy, Mao's misguided reforms resulted in a loss of credibility compounded by his advancing age. As a result, dissenting political factions within the Communist party threatened Mao's leadership. To regain political merit, Mao sought to undermine the high-ranking party leaders, Liu Shaoqi and Deng Xiaoping, through the Great Proletarian Cultural Revolution. In May 1966, the party formally introduced the May Sixteenth Circular, a document denouncing party members who allegedly strayed from the revolutionary path to embrace Western capitalism. An excerpt from the circular reads:

> The representatives of the capitalist class who have infiltrated our party, our government, our armed forces, and various cultural groups are actually a batch of counter-revolutionary revisionists. When the time is right, they will try to seize power, turning the dictatorship of the proletariat into one of the capitalist class. Some of these people have already been exposed by us, some have not, and some are still in our trust being groomed as our successors. They are Khrushchev types and they are sleeping right next to us. All levels of party cadres must be especially aware of this point.

The May 16 circular also introduced the newly established central Cultural Revolution Small Group (CRSG) made up of Mao's coterie of sympathizers, including Chen Boda, Kang Sheng, Jiang Qing, Wang Renzhong, Liu Zhijian, Zhang Chunqiao, Wang Li, Guan Feng, Qi Benyu, and Yao Wenyuan. While Liu and Deng anticipated a routine campaign, Mao, directing the CRSG, plotted their undoing.

To truly operationalize the Cultural Revolution, however, Mao needed the popular support or at least the semblance of support that he enjoyed during the 1949 revolution. However, by 1966 Mao's political rivals controlled the official media. To circumvent the official media, Mao capitalized on alternative venues, namely, big-character posters and China's youth, a revered conglomerate for dissent. Poon explains:

> The establishment of rival apparatus to the existing propaganda department was essential before the power seizure campaign could be carried out effectively by the Maoists. They finally selected the young Red Guards as the counterpart to the official propagandists, and they also decided to use *dazibao* as their primary

medium to compete with their official media. (Poon 1978:193)

In a tactical decision, Mao left Beijing for six months, distancing himself from party leadership. Directing his newly formed allies from a distance, he targeted Beijing University (Beida) to kindle the flames of the revolution, most memorably through the manufacture of a big-character poster, principally authored by Beida professor Nie Yuanzi. The Maoist clique simultaneously sanctified the big-character posters at Beida and legitimated big-character posters as a supreme medium of expression and agitation through a *People's Daily* editorial:

> The great Proletarian Cultural Revolution is now in full spate. We must stand at the forefront of this movement and actively guide it. It is necessary to arouse the masses without reservation and adopt the method of full and frank expression of views and opinions, of putting up posters written in big characters and of carrying out great debates. It is necessary to let the masses speak out fully, expose all the representatives of the bourgeoisie who oppose the Communist Party, socialism, and Mao Zedong's thought, expose all the monsters and, one by one, smash to pieces the reactionary bastions of the bourgeoisie. Chairman Mao Zedong says: "Posters written in big characters are an extremely useful new type of weapon." The revolutionary big-character posters are very good! They are "magic mirrors" to show up the monsters of all kinds. With everybody putting up such posters, it is possible, quickly and from all sides, to reveal the true face of the sinister anti-Party and anti-socialist gangs. These posters set out all kinds of opinions and bring out all

kinds of contradictions. And through these opinions and contradictions we should come to understand the situation and discover and solve the problems. By presenting the cardinal issues of right and wrong and getting everybody to discuss, examine, appraise, and criticize them, the revolutionary big-character posters concentrate in a single day twenty years' education of the masses, particularly in raising the proletarian consciousness of the younger generation. . . . The attitude toward these revolutionary posters is an important yardstick in the current great Cultural Revolution by which to differentiate genuine from sham revolutionaries and proletarian revolutionaries from bourgeois royalists. Are you a revolutionary? Then you are bound to welcome these posters, stand up for them, take a lead in writing them and encourage the masses to write them freely and expose the problems freely. Are you a royalist? Then you are bound to be scared to death of such posters. You will turn pale with fear and come out in a cold sweat at the sight of them, and in every possible way you will try to suppress the posters put up by the masses. Fear of the big-character posters means fear of the masses, fear of the revolution, fear of people's democracy, fear of the dictatorship of the proletariat. ("Revolutionary Big-Character Posters Are 'Magic Mirrors' That Show Up All Monsters," *People's Daily,* 1966)

Such official license resulted in a surge of big-character posters denouncing "feudal remnants" (*fengjian canyu*) on college campuses throughout China. With big-character posters as their weapons, students and faculty proclaimed to be the Red Guards of the new revolution. As the Cultural Revolution progressed, big-character posters became a critical means of information necessary for political survival during the Cultural Revolution. Big-character posters replaced official news media, broadcasting political shifts that dictated the correctness of one's actions and sympathies.

In response to Liu and Deng's growing concerns, Mao adopted a lackadaisical attitude. Under the illusion of Mao's support, Liu dispatched work teams to universities to quell student unrest. By covertly encouraging Liu's decision to send work teams to handle the growing agitation, Mao conveniently poised Liu as an authoritarian reactionary. Meanwhile, in his absence, Mao's image grew. Media coverage on his swim in the Yangtze River pointedly communicated both Mao's personal strength and his political vigor. Editorials commonly detailed both the size of the Yangtze and Mao's reluctance to rest during the swim; they drew parallels between the river and counter-revolutionary forces such as imperialism ("Chairman Mao Swims in the Yangtze," 1966).

Upon his return to Beijing in August 1966, Mao formalized his attack upon Liu Shaoqi. He criticized Liu's dispatch of work teams. He also wrote his famous big-character poster "Bombard the Headquarters" (*paoda silingbu*), attacking Liu Xiaoqi and further urging China's youth to rebel:

China's first Marxist-Leninist big-character poster and Commentator's article on it in *Renmin Ribao* [*People's Daily*] are indeed superbly written! Comrades, please read them again. But in the last fifty days or so some leading comrades from the central down to the local levels have acted in a diametrically opposite way. Adopting the reactionary stand of the bourgeoisie, they have enforced a bourgeois dictatorship and struck down the surging movement of the great Cultural Revolution of the proletariat. They have stood facts on their head and juggled black and white, encircled and suppressed revolutionaries, stifled opinions differing from their own, imposed a white terror, and felt very pleased with themselves. They have puffed up the arrogance of the bourgeoisie and deflated the morale of the proletariat. How poisonous! Viewed in connection with the Right deviation in 1962 and the wrong tendency of 1964 which was "Left" in form but Right in essence, shouldn't this make one wide awake?

Soon after Mao's big-character poster, the Central Committee formally initiated the Cultural Revolution. Liu Shaoqi was expelled and formally replaced by defense minister and People's Liberation Army commander Lin Biao. Mao's installation of Lin Biao enhanced the CRSG's authority, and the combined forces of Lin and the CRSG manipulated the course of the revolution.

The Lin Biao Chapter

The installation of Lin marked a new and compelling synergy between Mao and the People's Liberation Army (PLA), as well as between Mao and Lin himself. The media reproduced the Lin/Mao association in myriad ways. Publicity surrounding Mao constantly featured Lin at his side. Mao's political ambitions necessitated PLA support. At the same time, Lin Biao's political strategy included the radical exploitation of Mao's thought and image. Beginning in the early 1960s, Lin marketed Mao Zedong's thoughts through a series of articles. For example, in an open letter on the study of Mao's ideas, Lin stated:

China is a great socialist state of the dictatorship of the proletariat and has a population of seven hundred million. It needs a unifying thought, revolutionary thought, correct thought. That is Mao Zedong's thought. Only with this thought can we maintain vigorous revolutionary drive and keep firmly to the correct political orientation. ("Lin Biao on the Study of Mao's Works," 1970)

Headlines in the official press during the spring and summer of 1966 are telling: "Hold High the Great Banner of Mao Zedong's Thought and Actively Participate in the Great Socialist Cultural Revolution"; "Hold High the Great Red Banner of the Thought of Mao Zedong, Carry the Great Proletarian Cultural Revolution through to the End"; "Turn Our Army into a Great School in Mao Zedong's Thought." Lin's most memorable propagation of Mao's thought came in the form of the Little Red Book, or *Quotations from Chairman Mao*, a haphazard collection of quotes from Mao's speeches and writings. Having published the Little Red Book in 1964 to indoctrinate PLA soldiers, Lin reprinted the book in 1966 with a foreword indicative of his escalating praise of Mao's thought:

The most fundamental task for the political and ideological work of our Party is always to hold high the great red banner of Mao Zedong's thought, to arm the minds of the people throughout the country with Mao Zedong's thought, and to persist in putting Mao Zedong's thought in command of all work. The broad masses of the workers, the peasants, and the soldiers and the broad ranks of the revolutionary cadres and the revolutionary intellectuals must genuinely grasp Mao Zedong's thought and see to it that everyone studies Chairman Mao's writings, follows his teachings, acts according to his instructions, and becomes a good soldier of Chairman Mao's." (Foreword to the second edition of the Little Red Book, 1966)

As a result of Lin's patronage, the Chinese digested the Little Red Book with fervor. Lin passionately exhorted the importance of Mao's philosophy as a basis for all study, thought, and action. He reduced the price of the book and printed approximately a billion copies in the first three years of the Cultural Revolution (along with 1.5 million copies of Mao's *Selected Works*). Lin's hard-fought campaign to aggrandize Mao to consolidate his own position in the top echelons of Mao's regime catalyzed the idolatry developed toward Mao during the Cultural Revolution.

Lin Biao's manic iconicization of Mao raised the stakes of creative propaganda by accentuating orthodoxy, one's internal belief, over orthopraxy, one's actions. The emphasis on orthodoxy attempted a complete introjection of political ideology that encouraged a collective concept of self. Rae Yang (1997:97) describes a lecture she received as a child during the Cultural Revolution on this "third layer of thoughts": "It is like a cancer hidden inside you. If you cover it up and keep it a secret, it will find the environment agreeable. It will grow and spread and proliferate! It will take you over and kill you!"

As the Cultural Revolution gained momentum, Mao's image transmutated from aging engineer of economic disaster to trusted revolutionary icon. The metamorphosis was neither accidental nor complete. Rather, the combined efforts of the CRSG and Lin Biao, guided by Mao, jump-started Mao's political capital through reliance on ever more innovative propaganda modes, such as Red Guard publications, mass rallies, the Little Red Book, *chuanlian* (the exchange of revolutionary experiences), and Mao badges.

Ascent of the Red Guards

In late June 1966, a big-character poster written by the Qinghua Middle School Red Guards set the tone for the role of all Red Guards in the revolution:

> Revolution is rebellion, and the soul of Mao Zedong thought is rebellion. We must pay special attention to "applying ourselves," that is to say, to pay special attention to "rebel" [*zaofan*]. To dare to think, to dare to speak, to dare to act, to dare to intrude, and to dare to revolt is, in one word, to dare to zaofan. This is the most precious quality of a proletarian revolutionary and the fundamental principle of the proletarian spirit! Not to zaofan is one hundred percent revisionism! . . . The revolutionary should emulate the Monkey King, brandishing his staff and using his mystical powers to shatter the old world and to send everyone and everything into chaos, the more chaos the better. (Yan and Gao 1996:58)

In early August, Mao publicly departed from Liu Shaoqi and responded to the zaofan spirit of the Qinghua Red Guards in a letter of support that signaled Mao's interest in escalating the activism of the Red Guards. On August 18, 1966, Mao organized a rally at Tiananmen Square to celebrate the launch of the Cultural Revolution and further mobilize the Red Guards, the first of eight such rallies. Approximately one million Red Guards attended from all over the country. During the rally, a student decorated Mao with a red armband, a sign of solidarity between Mao and the Red Guards. In its magnitude, the rally presented a powerful visual image of support and devotion directed toward Mao. An official editorial described the scene:

> At five o'clock in the morning when the sun had just risen above the eastern horizon and had begun shedding

its brilliant rays, Chairman Mao arrived at Tiananmen Square, which was covered by a vast sea of people and a forest of red flags. . . . The square was seething with excitement. Turning toward Chairman Mao, people raised their hands overhead and jumped up, cheered, and clapped. Many clapped till their hands became sore, many shed tears of joy. . . . A great many hands, holding red-covered *Quotations from Chairman Mao Zedong*, stretched toward the rostrum. A million warm hearts flew out to Chairman Mao, and a million pairs of eyes sparkling with revolutionary fervor were turned on him. ("Carry the Great Proletarian Cultural Revolution through to the End," 1966)

The August 18 rally marked a new phase of radical activism among Red Guards, who were energized by the proposed campaign to "destroy the four olds" (*po sijiu*)—ideas, culture, customs, and habits—to bring forth the new. The Red Guards of the number 2 middle school of Beijing delivered Mao's iconoclastic agenda in no uncertain terms:

We are the critics of the old world; we want to criticize and we want to crush all old thought, old culture, old customs, and old habits. All servers of the capitalists such as barbershops, tailor shops, photograph studios, used book stalls are to be included. We want to zaofan the old world. . . . The torrent of the Cultural Revolution is now flooding in upon every stronghold of the plutocrats of the capitalist class. The warm beds of the capitalist class can no longer be maintained! Odd hair styles such as "aeroplane" and "spiraling pagoda" and Hong Kong–style jeans and T-shirts, as well as pornographic pictures and publications, must be severely suppressed. We must think that such are small matters, yet the restoration of capitalism begins precisely in these small things. We must eradicate the warm bed and young buds of capitalism. We propose to the revolutionary workers in such professions as barbering, tailoring, and photography not to do Hong Kong–style haircuts, not to tailor to Hong Kong–style clothing, not to shoot lurid photographs, and not to sell pornographic publications. . . . We want to, in the shortest time possible, eliminate Hong Kong–style clothing, shave off strange-looking hair styles, and burn pornographic books and pictures. Cowboy pants should become short pants, with the leftover material saved for mending. "Rocket shoes" [sharply pointed boots] should be lopped off to become sandals. High-heeled shoes should be flattened. Bad books and pictures should be turned into waste material. . . . We want to interfere and we want to interfere to the very end. We must stop up every orifice leading to capitalism, and we must smash every incubator of revisionism. We will not be sentimental over this. (Yan and Gao 1996:65)

Red Guards interpreted and executed the four old campaigns with a violent fervor aimed at material property and, eventually, at individuals. Red Guards took advantage of the vagueness of the campaign's rhetoric, pilfering and demolishing public and private spheres with euphoric license. Efforts among Red Guards to revolutionize Chinese culture resulted in a carnival of the bizarre. In one of the more ambitious proposals, a group of Beijing middle school students posted a list of one hundred tasks to eliminate the old elements of society. Such elements included, but were not limited to, the national anthem, newspapers, perfumes, expendable movie scenes, private enterprise, blue jeans, slick hairdos, rocket shoes, tight pants, Hong Kong–style clothes, classical literature and art, toys, pets such as fish, cats, and dogs, pedicabs, public drinking games, magicians, circus performers, limousines, television, motorcycles, smoking, dirty jokes, nicknames, jewelry, lavish wedding ceremonies, sofas, gifts, and spring festival celebrations. Mao icons reigned supreme for the revolutionization of society, as evident in twenty of the hundred dictates (see "One Hundred Items for Destroying the Old and Establishing the New," 1970:215):

1. Under the charge of residential committees, every street must set up a quotation plaque; every household must have on its walls a picture of the Chairman plus quotations by Chairman Mao.

2. More quotations by Chairman Mao must be put up in the parks. Ticket takers on buses and conductors on trains should make the propagation of Mao Zedong thought and the reading of Chairman Mao's quotations their primary task.

3. The management bureaus of publishing enterprises must mainly print Chairman Mao's works, and most of the sales of New China bookstores must make the radiance of Mao Zedong thought shine in every corner of the whole country.

4. Printing companies must print quotations by the Chairman in large numbers; they must be sold in every bookstore until there is a copy of the *Quotations from Chairman Mao* in the hands of everyone in the whole country.

5. With a copy of the *Quotations from Chairman Mao* in the hands of everyone, each must carry it with him, constantly study it, and do everything in accord with it.

6. Fine art publishing companies must print large batches of stock quotations by the Chairman. Especially on anniversary occasions, they must sell great quantities of

quotations and revolutionary couplets—enough to satisfy the needs of the people.

7. Plaques of quotations by the Chairman must be hung on all available bicycles and pedicabs; pictures of the Chairman must be hung and Chairman Mao's sayings painted on motor vehicles and trains.

8. The relevant departments must manufacture bicycle and pedicab quotation plaques on a scale large enough to meet the needs of the people.

9. Newly manufactured products such as bicycles, motor vehicles, trains, airplanes, etc. must uniformly bear quotation plaques. This procedure must be increased, not decreased.

10. Neighborhood work must put Mao Zedong thought in first place, must set up small groups for the study of Chairman Mao's works, and must revolutionize housewives.

11. Every school and every unit must set up highest-directive propaganda teams so that everyone can hear at any time the repeated instructions of the Chairman.

12. Broadcasting units must be set up in every park and at every major intersection, and, under the organizational responsibility of such organs as the Red Guards, propagate Mao Zedong thought and current international and national events.

13. The old national anthem absolutely must be reformed by workers, peasants, and soldiers into a eulogy to the party and Chairman Mao.

14. From now on every newspaper must put Mao Zedong thought in first place. Editorials must be few and to the point, and there must be more good articles dealing with the living study and living application of the Chairman's works by the workers, peasants, and soldiers.

15. Letters and stamps must never have bourgeois things

printed on them (such as cats, dogs, or other artistic things). Politics must be predominant. A quotation by Chairman Mao or a militant utterance by a hero must be printed on every envelope.

16. Hereafter on the national day, everyone must carry a copy of the Chairman's quotations and a bouquet, and the bouquets must be arranged in slogans.

17. Shop windows cannot be dominated by displays of scents and perfumes. They must be decorated with simplicity and dignity and must put Mao Zedong thought first.

18. Theaters must have a strong political atmosphere. Before the movie starts, quotations from Chairman Mao must be shown. Don't let the bourgeoisie rule our stages. Cut the superfluous hooligan scenes, and reduce the price of tickets on behalf of the workers, peasants, and soldiers.

19. Literary and art workers must energetically model in clay heroic images of workers, peasants, and soldiers engaged in living study and living application of Chairman Mao's works. Their works must be pervaded by the one red line of Mao Zedong thought.

20. Schools must use Mao's works as textbooks and educate the youth in Mao Zedong thought.

Red Guards also called for the abolishment of any type of "bizarre bourgeois attire" (zichanjieji qi zhuang yifu). Individuals adopted androgynous attire, limiting clothing to gray and blue Mao suits and army-green uniforms. The new code of appearance forbade makeup, long hair, high heels, and dresses. Pants had to be appropriately baggy to pass muster by Red Guard overseers: "If there was not enough room for a soda bottle to drop down to the cuff, they would slit the legs up to the thigh" (Gao 1987:95). Gao remembers a local "criminal" paraded in a pink silk qipao

with red satin shoes around her neck with hair cut into a
"tangled haystack." One child, likewise, remembers Red
Guards parading her mother who was weighted with a
wooden board featuring a snake in a flashy dress, high heels,
large breasts, and the words, "I confess. I am a snake in the
disguise of a beautiful woman" (Wen 1995:161). A Beijing
respondent sums up the ambience:

> At the time, you could only wear things real simple.
> Green color was passable, because it was the color of
> the army. Many Red Guards borrowed their parents'
> clothes. There was one standard: you could not dress
> too fancy. For example, at the time, there were Red
> Guards stationed at Wangfujing. They had sticks in
> their hands. If they saw women wearing high heels,
> they would use the stick to hit off the heel on one of
> the shoes. They would not do both. If one of the heels
> was taken off, they would have to limp. If they saw
> women with long hair, the Red Guards would cut it
> off. They had scissors in their hands. Wearing skirts
> was impossible. At that time, people all followed the
> unspoken rule.

The new code of the Red Guards saturated the Chinese
population with a fervor that left no one unscathed, rapidly
and superficially revolutionizing the public sphere. Individuals changed their names; among the more common changes
were the words for defending Mao Zedong (*Weidong*), in-
heriting red (*Jihong*), permanent revolution (*Yongge*). East-
Is-Red Boulevard and Anti-Imperialism Road became
common names for thoroughfares. In one of the more out-
landish propositions (one that has became an urban legend
in much of Cultural Revolution literature), Red Guards demanded the reversal of street lights, arguing that red, not
green, should represent advancement. In a response that

reflected his tactical genius, Zhou Enlai claimed that studies proved that the color red caught drivers' attention, and, therefore, red lights could be interpreted as safeguarding revolutionaries (Yan and Gao 1996).

At the third Red Guard rally in September 1966, the party explicitly supported Red Guard actions, as is clear in the following excerpt of Lin Biao's speech:

> Red Guard fighters, revolutionary students, the general orientation of your struggle has always been correct. Chairman Mao and the Party's Central Committee support you! So do the broad masses of workers, peasants, and soldiers! Your revolutionary actions have shaken the whole of society and given a blow to the dregs and remnant evil elements from the old world. You have scored brilliant successes in the vigorous fight to destroy the four olds and foster the four news. You have created utter consternation among those in authority who are taking the capitalist road, the reactionary bourgeois "authorities" and bloodsuckers and parasites. You have acted correctly and done well! ("Carry the Great Proletarian Cultural Revolution through to the End," 1996)

Mao's consecration of Red Guard activities via the mass rallies at Tiananmen roused Red Guards from all over the country to travel to Beijing, for *chuanlian*, or the "exchange of revolutionary experiences." The party not only sanctioned the movement but also offered the incentive of free travel throughout the country.

Xuetong lun

The timely mobilization of the Red Guards provided an outlet for students frustrated with a system of political advancement based on one's proximity to revolutionary leaders. This "bloodline theory" (*xuetong lun*) prescribed legitimate political status only to members of the correct political lineage, the "five red categories" (*hong wulei*), including workers, peasants, cadres, revolutionary heroes, and revolutionary intellectuals. At the beginning of the Cultural Revolution, Red Guards proudly promoted this pedigree definition of status. Red Guards excluded anyone without a red background and directed their attacks against members of the "five black categories" (*hei wulei*), including landlords, wealthy peasants, bad elements, counter-revolutionaries, and rightists. Such categorizations resulted in an "estate-like social structure" (A. Chan 1992) that took on dramatic implications as students divided into categories according to their heritage and were persecuted or rewarded accordingly. Long envious of their classmates who attained similar educational privileges through their intellect (rather than "good breeding"), Red Guards asserted their new domination with a vengeance.

Red Guards understood an innate sense of superiority by virtue of the fact that they were "born red" (*zilaihong*). A couplet that emerged from an elite middle school came to stand as the early Red Guard motto: "If the father is a hero, the son will be a brave man. If the father is a reactionary, the son will be a scoundrel" (*laozi yingxiong er haohan, laozi fandong er hundan*).

More extreme versions of the couplet abounded. Zhoujing, son of an intellectual, remembers being chided by children on the playground during the Cultural Revolution: "Dog, dog, capitalist dog. The father is a big dog. The son is a little one" (Wen 1995:140). Zhai (1992) bases her writing on her ascent (and eventual downfall) within the Red Guard movement as the offspring of a "red birth." She regretfully remembers her advocacy of the bloodline theory, encouraged by the words of other "red" members of her class: "We are born red! The red comes with us from our mothers' wombs. And I say right here you are born black! What can you do about us?" (Zhai 1992:81). Such admonitions developed into a song created by her clique:

> The old man a true man, the son is a hero,
> The old man a reactionary, the son is an asshole.
> If you are revolutionary, then step forward and come
>   along.
> If you are not, damn you to hell.

The intensity surrounding the bloodline theory reached fever pitch as Red Guards beat, tortured, and killed members of the five black categories. The "red terror" (*hongse kongbu*) represented the height of Red Guard brutality. During this time, Red Guards established their own "reformatories," where members of the black categories underwent merciless punishment, including kneeling on cinders (*guimeizha*), face painting (*youqi tulian*), experimental hangings (*shangdiao shiyan*), loud kowtows (*kouxiangtou*, banging one's head roughly on the ground), riding in an airplane (*zuofeiji*, bending one's body forward with arms outstretched backward), hair burning (*huoshao toufa*), knifing of the buttocks (*daoduo pigu*), boiling waterbaths (*kaishui xizao*), target practice (*daba*), sudden lancing (*tuci*), and sweeping of the lower legs (*saotangtui*) (Yan and Gao 1996:82).

At the beginning of the Red Guard mobilization, students who had less of a pure blood heritage did not challenge the exclusionary rules of Red Guard membership. However, in the fall of 1966, Mao officially disputed the bloodline theory, thereby broadening the base of redness. While "bad seeds" could not be reborn red, they could now elevate their status through political participation despite a bad family background. Mao's motivations were political:

he realized that the children of the cadre who constituted the Red Guard movement were much less apt to challenge authorities at the highest levels (Chan 1985). Out-circle students engaged in chuanlian, their presence fracturing the exclusive authority of the Red Guards. Personal communications among chuanlian participants disturbed the unity of highly politicized categories, particularly as those participants became more diversified.

The chaos that resulted with chuanlian diminished whatever illusions Mao may have harbored about nationalizing the revolution. The mass mobility crippled production and transportation. The exchange also heightened the misguided vigor of the Red Guards, most memorably through an incident at Confucius's birthplace, where Red Guards covered buildings, homes, and streets with red paint to create a "red sea." The party admonished the perpetrators in an official notice:

According to the reactions of the masses of various places, some municipal party and official units, on the pretext of recording the sayings of Chairman Mao and of "beautifying the city aspects," have enthusiastically entered into "red sea" activities—that is, using red paint to cover doors and large wall surfaces and even forcing every household to pay up. In some villages, in addition to red sea action, there were even attempts at "big edifices." Then there are the otherwise-motivated capitalist-roaders still in power and those in support of the capitalist reactionary line who would take advantage of such activities to deprive the masses from posting their own posters. Such was their way of covering up their own crimes against Mao Zedong thought. This method of theirs not only completely disobeys the way of diligent frugality long taught by Comrade

Mao Zedong, but also constitutes the base action of showing resistance to big-character posters and to the Great Proletarian Cultural Revolution. The Central Committee is of the view that every level of leadership must resolutely put a stop to such erroneous methods. (Yan and Gao 1996:90)

To relieve the transportation debacle caused by the revolutionary exchange, the party halted the Red Guard rallies and directed Red Guards to travel back to their homes to share their experiences—by foot. The party framed their directive to travel by foot as a second long march, in the footsteps of the revolutionary forefathers. The historical association held obvious appeal to the young agitators; however, it was a slow, cold, and long trek back home. Others ignored the government's orders and continued to travel.

During the winter of 1966 through 1967, rebels organized independent factions to challenge the conservative Red Guards. This division resulted in uncontrolled political infighting that led to armed conflicts and, eventually, to their state-enforced dissolution. In January 1967, rebels undertook a "power seizure" in which they were directed by Mao to overthrow high-ranking and local officials and seize power for themselves. By initiating the power seizures, Mao intended to demolish the existing power structure and rebuild the party. However, the unprecedented struggle to seize power resulted in an escalation of factional fighting among the Guards.

In the summer of 1967, Mao urged the Red Guard factions to unify in "great alliances." However, cleavages between them were enormous. The mass organizations maintained entrenchment camps and had begun to stockpile arsenals of weapons, ignoring party orders to cease fighting. Mao's plan to establish government-sponsored revolutionary committees to replace former power holders lost ground with every day of continued fighting. Party leaders summoned representatives from opposing factions to Beijing to negotiate alliances. The party changed its public tone regarding the mass organizations, going to sometimes humorous lengths to reconceptualize the divided groups. For example, rebels who seized power in Anhui in January 1967 declared their actions as very good (*hao de hen*), resulting in their self-ascribed nickname, *hao pai*. The conservative Guards responded with the taunt that the rebels' actions were as good as a fart (*hao ge pi*). Mao's insistence upon no longer using the factional names of rebels and conservatives led authorities to refer to the two groups in negotiation proceedings as the good faction and the fart faction (Barnouin and Yu 1993).

Frustrated by the resistance of Red Guard factions to unify, Mao dispatched the PLA to schools to establish revolutionary committees to restore order. A more aggressive yoke to Red Guard activism followed when Mao initiated the rustification movement, whereby he ordered China's youth to work in the countryside to learn revolution from the peasants. During the next ten years, the government relocated more than sixteen million urban youths to rural areas.

In addition to suppressing the Red Guards and establishing revolutionary committees, the government initiated an intensive new wave of political ritual to redirect political energies best characterized by the three loyalties and four boundlesses campaign. The three loyalties included loyalty to Chairman Mao, loyalty to Mao's thought, and loyalty to his revolutionary line. The four boundlesses referred to love for Chairman Mao, his thought, his proletarian revolutionary line, and the proletarian revolutionary headquarters. During this time, the ritualization of Mao's image reached its height and saturated every aspect of one's life. Mao's portrait was displayed everywhere, and all families dutifully "invited portraits of Chairman Mao into their homes" (qing Mao zhuxi xiang jinwu). Mao's presence inundated everyday life, as is evident in the process of morning resolutions and nightly reports in front of the Chairman's portrait. One Red Guard recalls entering a room in her home, barely recognizing the surroundings:

> I remember the moment my father took my sister Xiaoming and myself into our living room. On the central wall, where a classical Chinese painting had hung, was now a portrait of Chairman Mao. The classical Chinese poems by artists known for their calligraphy that had flanked the painting were also missing, replaced by cheap prints of Mao's quotations in his script. I still remember the two of them: "Serve the people heart and soul," and "Fight selfishness. Repudiate revisionism." My father took my younger sister's hand and mine in his. Standing between us in front of the portrait of Mao, he said quietly to Mao's portrait, "Trust the Party. Trust the masses." (Wen 1995:78)

One student describes her newly reopened classroom during this time:

> There were no chairs, no notebooks, no books, although Mao's Little Red Book was in plentiful supply. Nothing, however, could dampen my eagerness which was rewarded each day with something new. Professor Yang taught us a new song: "The East is red, the sun rises, China brought forth a Mao Zedong. He devotes himself to his people, he is the great star of our redemption." On Saturday in front of an effigy of Mao, the gym teacher had us practice the steps of a dance sym-

bolizing "loyalty." The art teacher taught us how to paint a large red sun with gigantic golden rays under which we learned to write, "Long Live Mao." (Niu-Niu 1995:61)

Gao provides the most detailed nuances of the movement, including the obligatory loyalty dances and the duty to report on one's behavior twice daily to Mao's portrait. His narrative expresses relief from the heated Red Guard battles as well as the relaxation that came with public ritualization:

The campaign consisted of decorating our classrooms, reciting Chairman Mao's quotations and three most-read articles, and declaring our love and loyalty. Class 85 put a poster of Chairman Mao in an army uniform on the back wall. Underneath, we painted ocean waves and ships, and a radiant red sun rising on the horizon. . . . Every morning, we assembled before Chairman Mao, raised our little red books above our heads, and chanted "wishing our great leader Chairman Mao an infinitely long life, and his close comrade-in-arms good health forever!" We would sing the song "sailing on the sea depends on the helmsman." Then we would read quotations in accordance with the day's agenda. . . . Every evening before bedtime, we assembled again to sing, chant, wave our red books, and report to Chairman Mao about what we had done during the day. These routines at the start and end of the day were called "asking for instructions in the morning and reporting back in the evening." The campaign grew more creative and varied. Chairman Mao quotation contests became popular. Caolan recited two hundred and seventy pages of the red book without missing a word. Xiangyun could recite any quotation as soon as you gave her the page number and category. I did not do very well at quotations, but impressed people with my flawless recitation of all thirty-seven of Chairman Mao's published poems. Dances were another way to express our loyalty. The most popular one was set to a Tibetan tune, "On the golden hill of Beijing." The campaign led to a movement to "revolutionize daily life." It consisted of replacing daily talk with quotations from Chairman Mao. When you got out of bed in the morning, instead of saying, "let's get up," you said, "carry the revolution through to the end." When you went to bed, you said, "never forget class struggle." People greeted each other with "serve the people." If you bought anything, be it a movie or bottle of soy sauce, you had to initiate the transaction with a quotation. This was troublesome for older people with poor memories, but nobody protested. One had to sacrifice some personal convenience for the sake of making revolution. Chairman Mao quotations were useful in many situations. In the marketplace one day, I heard a housewife and a saleswoman trading quotations at a vegetable stall. The housewife was choosing tomatoes with great care, examining each one, since they were expensive in the winter. The displeased sales clerk said, "Fight selfishness and repudiate revisionism." The housewife replied, "We communists pay great attention to conscientiousness." They quoted back and forth until they were ready for a fight. Onlookers used quotations to stop them. The three loyalties and four boundless loves campaign was a positive development as far as I was concerned. Carrying it out took precedence over the antagonisms between us and our east-is-red corps classmates. The cessation of torture next door allowed us much more sleep. We no longer had to be on the defensive every minute of the night and day. (Gao 1987:317)

Chang also reflects on the acceleration of political ritual during this time, though in a more cynical tone. Despite her obvious resentment over the maddening rituals, Chang remembers being able to laugh for the first time in a long while.

Grotesque forms of worshipping Mao had been part of our lives for some time—chanting, wearing Mao badges, waving the little red book. But the idolatry had escalated when the revolutionary committees were formally established nationwide by 1968. The committee members reckoned that the safest and most rewarding course of action was to do nothing, except promote the worship of Mao—and, of course, to engage in political persecutions. Once, in a pharmacy in Chengdu, an old shop assistant with a pair of impassive eyes behind gray-rimmed spectacles murmured without looking at me, "when sailing the seas we need a helmsman. . . ." There was a pregnant pause. It took me a moment to realize I was supposed to complete the sentence, which was a fawning quotation from Lin Biao about Mao. Such exchanges had just been enforced as a standard greeting. I had to mumble, "when making revolution we need Mao Zedong thought." Revolutionary committees all over China ordered statues of Mao to be built. A huge white marble figure was planned for the center of Chengdu. . . . Specialty trucks called loyalty trucks were shipping the marble out from the mountains. These trucks were decorated like floats in a parade, festooned with red silk ribbons and a huge silk flower in front. . . . After we said goodbye to the driver who had brought us from Chengdu we hitched a lift on one of these loyalty trucks for the last stretch to Ningnan. On the way we stopped at a marble quarry for a rest. A group of sweating workers, naked to the waist, were drinking tea and smoking their yard-long pipes. One of them told us they were not using any machinery, as only working with their bare hands could express their loyalty to Mao. I was horrified to see a badge pinned to his bare chest. When we were back in the truck, Jin-ming observed that the badge must have been stuck on with plaster. And, as for their devoted quarrying by hand: "They probably don't have any machines in the first place." (Chang 1991:399)

The Ninth Party Congress in April 1969 formalized Lin Biao as Mao's successor and declared the Cultural Revolution a success. At the Ninth Congress, Mao anticipated that the Cultural Revolution would reach its finale in another year. His prediction was well off the mark.

Seven years and many brutal campaigns later, Mao died, and the Cultural Revolution officially ended. Purged officials reestablished themselves in the party structure and arrested the Gang of Four, including Mao's wife, Jiang Qing, and sympathizers Zhang Chunqiao, Wang Hongwen, and Yao Wenyuan. The party enshrined Mao's body in a crystal coffin and built a mausoleum, where his body has been on display ever since.

2

Manufacturing

Mao

Within the context of China's expansive symbolic culture, the badge, or *zhang*, embodies a conceptual richness that transcends decoration and connotes a form of affiliation or identification. In fact, Li (1993) asserts that the character for zhang, translated today as "badge," was initially used to refer to a flag. The Qin army used such flags for both identification and subterfuge; to disguise their identity, soldiers changed flags (Li 1993).

The Mao portrait badge, or *Mao xiangzhang*, shows Mao's centered portrait. The mass production of Mao badges during the Cultural Revolution was based on a prestigious history. Though Mao badges attained their highest levels of production and distribution during the Cultural Revolution, they had already existed at least three decades earlier. They emphasize Mao's authority through his portrait, or likeness, and maintain the spirit of affiliation, authority, and appropriation in strikingly inventive ways.

Yenan Badges

As early as the 1930s, students at the Anti-Japanese University manipulated empty toothpaste tubes to create badges featuring Mao, Marx, Engels, Lenin, and Stalin. Communist soldiers fighting the Japanese wore Mao badges. One of the earliest Mao badges, a small, wooden, hand-carved badge—still in existence today—surfaced among the remains of a Chinese soldier who died in battle (Zhou 1993).

During the Yenan period, up-and-coming Communists decorated party conferences with portraits of Mao, Marx, Lenin, Stalin, and the revolutionary general Zhu De, painted on white cloth and hung on the wall. Communists also created badges with Mao's portrait as both a political statement and commemoration of their successes. They reproduced large numbers of stamps and badges with Mao's image in honor of the Seventh National Congress, held in Yenan in 1945. Within this genre, a teacher at the Lushun art academy named Ling Zifeng created a finely sculpted model to produce Mao badges as gifts to members of the Seventh Congress. A contemporary memorial to Ling features his badge contribution:

"I love the beautiful world." This is the last word Ling Zifeng left with us. Ling Zifeng, one of the new Chinese film founders, an exemplary Communist of the Chinese Communist Party, a world famous filmmaker and artist of high prestige, versatile talents and unique style, and a director of the Beijing Film Studio, died of cancer at the age of eighty-two, at 8:05 A.M. on March 2, 1999, in Beijing. . . . To celebrate the convening of the seventh National Congress of the Communist Party of China, Ling Zifeng spent only one night finishing, carving, and casting the first Mao Zedong badge in China. The original mold of the badge was collected by Premier Zhou Enlai. The one which Chen Yi wore is still collected in the Chinese Revolutionary Museum. . . . During the seventeen years from 1949 to the

Cultural Revolution, Ling made a large number of films with great enthusiasm and might. . . . During the ten years' Cultural Revolution, Ling Zifeng suffered persecution and was put under detention. Later he was transferred to the May seventh cadre school to be reformed through labor. It left him with ten years' gap in artistic creation.

This particular set of badges by Ling Zifeng—one of them now on display at the museum of the Chinese Revolution—reflects the process of delicate craftsmanship involved in the early re-creation of Mao's image. Ling carved Mao's portrait, borrowed from an existing Mao badge, with a fruit knife into an inkstand. He then poured liquefied tin into the carving and, when set, encased the series in elaborate red boxes stating, "a gift for the seventh national conference by Yenan Lushun fine arts institute" (Zhou 1993). To show his gratitude for the badge, Zhou Enlai purportedly visited the institute and received the inkstand as a gift; it no longer exists. Students at the Lushun Art Academy produced other designs for the Seventh Congress, including a frontal photograph of Mao with parted hair on a white background, and a photograph of Mao with hair combed back on a red background (Xu 1993).

Badges also commemorated Yenan meetings centered on the Shaanxi-Gansu-Ningxia border area in 1944 and 1945. These badge designs included Mao's frontal profile and Mao with Zhu De. Both badge designs were rectangular in shape, approximately two by three centimeters in size (Xu 1993).

Yenan University students created a school badge adopting Mao's profile while he made a speech to university students. The school badge was rectangular, one centimeter wide and three centimeters long. Yenan graduates later created more generalized tin Mao badges (Xu 1993).

Although we don't know just how many badges were made during the Yenan period, Xu (1993) claims that no more than ten different designs were created. Most of these badges used photographs of Mao and commemorative slogans, unlike the later trend of using political proclamations. Yenan badges were typically hand-made and were of limited production and distribution (Xu 1993).

Postliberation Badges

The Chinese Communist Party reproduced Mao's image more intensively following the establishment of the People's Republic in 1949. Manufacturers created and circulated badge models, which involved the use of various metals. The themes became more varied although they remained primarily commemorative.

Establishment badges made of red copper marked the gathering in Tiananmen Square on October 1949 that celebrated the announcement of the People's Republic. A five-star red flag and the Central Communist Party (CCP) flag depicting a sickle and ax waving over Tiananmen are on top of the badges. Pictures of wheat and ribbons decorate the sides. The bottom of these badges includes a half circle of Chinese characters, stating "in memory of the establishment of the People's Republic of China." Mao Zedong's portrait was not added to establishment badges until 1951.

Among the more popular badges of the postliberation period were those made in support of the War to Resist U.S. Aggression and Aid Korea. The CCP circulated these friendship badges among Chinese soldiers in Korea and Korean citizens. People's Liberation Army (PLA) soldiers returning from the Korean War received five-star-shaped military-achievement badges with Mao's portrait in the middle and a peace dove on the back. These badges were typically made of yellow copper with characters reading "in memory of the anti-American Korean War" inscribed on them. During the Korean War, the Chinese people's appreciation delegation visited soldiers in Korea, bearing gift packages. Among the necessities were military postcards, cigarettes, teacups, and towels, in addition to appreciation notebooks with Mao badges inserted on the front cover (Zhou 1993). A veteran of the Korean War offers an offbeat anecdote of Mao badge incentives during the time:

> In the summer of 1953, the peace talks were going pretty good and things were going a little better in the camp. . . . One morning, we noticed a Chinese guard over in the corner with a fly swatter. We watched him and he would swat a fly, pick it up and put it in a little envelope. Pretty soon, he would swat another fly and put that in an envelope. They were always doing some strange things so we didn't pay much attention to him. But the next day, we saw another guard swatting flies and doing the same thing. Now our curiosity got the best of us so we asked one of the camp instructors what they were doing. He told us that they have a fly killing project and they were going to make China the most fly-free country in the world. He stated that it was the duty of citizen, soldier, student, everyone to participate. We recalled that a few years before, they had a starling killing campaign as the starlings were eating all the grain in the fields. So they waged this war and killed all the starlings only to find out that the insects now were eating all the grain. . . . O.K., now they were going to kill flies, and we asked the instructor why they were saving the dead flies? He told us that as an incentive, everybody gets points for the number of flies they turn in. They were working to get enough points

to receive a Mao Zedong badge from the camp commander. . . . A few days later at the morning formation, it was announced that any one of us who would like to participate in this campaign could participate on a voluntary basis, you just raise your hands and they would be issued a fly swatter. He also announced that as an incentive to kill flies, they would give that man a factory-made cigarette for every two hundred flies turned in. . . . The next day everybody was swatting flies and saving them. . . . The Chinese did keep their word and we started to get a real cigarette.

Sino-Soviet friendship badges were also popular during the post-liberation period. Following the establishment of the Sino-Soviet friendship associations in both the People's Republic of China and the Soviet Union, active participants in branch associations created and received commemorative badges. After 1958, when Sino-Soviet relations worsened, many Chinese destroyed these friendship badges, so not many are available today (Zhou 1993).

Badges also celebrated more provincial agendas, including Tibetan "liberation," socialist construction projects, and government delegations to the people. In May 1961, the CCP signed a treaty marking Tibet's peaceful liberation. On the twenty-fifth anniversary of the People's Liberation Army in August 1952, each member of the PLA involved in Tibetan liberation received a five-star military-achievement badge with Mao's portrait. With the establishment of the PLA in Tibet, soldiers distributed military-achievement Mao badges among Tibetans to promote goodwill (Zhou 1993).

Badges were also created to praise major socialist development projects such as the construction of the Xian hydraulic power station. This power station, completed in four years, became an important resource for agricultural irrigation and industrial production for Shanghai and the Yangtze Delta region. During the opening ceremony for the station in December 1963, the CCP distributed souvenir badges with Mao's portrait surrounded by sunshine over a model of a large dam. Zhou Enlai's quotation, in typical nationalist style, marks the back: "Celebrate the victorious construction of the very first hydraulic station designed and constructed by our whole country" (Zhou 1993).

Badge production by various Chinese universities increased following liberation. The Anti-Japanese University made Mao badges for graduating students. Guangzhou University produced one of the more unique early badge sets that included three pieces. The first bore the school emblem, with Mao Zedong's portrait on the left and the school motto on the right: "Honesty, unity, simplicity, love, diligence, and bravery." The second badge pictured Mao, with characters stating, "Be a good servant to the people; be a good student." This badge was given to academically high-achieving students. The third badge was a graduation badge with Mao's portrait and a flag design (Li 1993; Zhou 1993).

It was customary for the CCP to reward model workers, soldiers, and students with Mao badges. For example, the Anting region food production system awarded productive workers with a badge featuring Mao's portrait skirted by a sunrise. In the early 1960s, the military distributed "five good soldiers" Mao badges, followed by the government production of "five good workers" badges (Zhou 1993).

As early as 1950, factories marketed Mao badges on a limited scale for the popular public. For example, the Shanghai Gold-Work Manufacturers made twenty-two-karat-gold Mao badges—eventually responding to the scarcity of resources by downsizing to thirteen karats—and silver badges. The factory advertised the badges in the *People's Daily*, February 10, 1953, for about seven hundred dollars (Zhou 1993).

Interestingly, most owners of these badges eventually exchanged them for gold jewelry, so the badges are quite rare
today (Li 1993). One Shanghai collector still owns a five-
star gold-mounted badge. The five stars are made of silver,
surrounding a twenty-two-karat-gold portrait of Mao and
Stalin. The back of the badge reads: "Shanghai Gold-worker
Manufacturers" (Zhou 1993).

Cultural Revolution Badges

Mao badges are typically associated with the Cultural Revolution, a time when the government and the
people produced, distributed, and consumed Mao's image
on a massive scale. When Mao received the people's representatives in Beijing on August 10, 1966, some representatives wore the earliest version of the Cultural Revolution
Mao badge—a small, round badge with Mao's profile on a
red background. On August 18, 1966, Red Guards presented
Mao with a number of badge variations. At the fifth meeting with Red Guards on October 18, Lin Biao and Zhou Enlai
both donned Mao badges. By December 26, 1966, Lin Biao's
wife, an avid badge collector, displayed a vast and diverse
private collection obtained through gifts and her own collecting activity (Li 1993).

Beijing Red Flag Badge Factory and Shanghai United
Badge Factory produced the first Cultural Revolution Mao
badges. According to Zhou (1993), Shanghai's badge factory
had produced at least one million badges by September 1967.
One badge collector remembers when the Beijing Red Flag
Badge Factory distributed the first badges at Xinhua bookstore in 1966. According to this respondent, lines of people
formed on Wangfujing throughout the night in anticipation
of getting a badge when the bookstore opened in the morning. He describes the atmosphere: "Everybody at the time

was wearing the badges. If you look at your family album at all the pictures taken during the Cultural Revolution, you see people wearing Mao badges."

The Chinese public consumed the badges voraciously, and manufacturers struggled to meet the demand for them. Badge factories celebrated new designs with street parades, complete with drums, red flags, and factory employees wearing the badges (Zhou 1993). Premier weeklies published during the Cultural Revolution abound with testimonials of the people's enthusiasm for Mao propaganda. A typical letter reads: "In the days and nights to come, we cannot depart from Mao Zedong's thought even for a second. We especially long for a shining badge of Chairman Mao so that in the hard struggle ahead of us we can draw strength and courage from it" ("World's People Eagerly Seek Chairman Mao Badges," 1968:2).

This enthusiasm reportedly transcended national, or at least Third World, boundaries. For example, one weekly relays a story about a Burmese woman who lost her Mao badge. Her father, sympathetic about her loss, allegedly searched for hours to find the badge, then walked five kilometers to his daughter's work to give it to her. She reportedly exclaimed, "This is my most precious treasure. I never want to be without it shining upon my breast" ("Peoples of the World Love Chairman Mao," 1968:26).

Propaganda workers lost sleep and mealtimes in their efforts to reproduce Mao's image. Reportedly haunted by lines of waiting consumers outside of a Mao book publishing house, factory workers left their homes (and beds) in the middle of winter to return to the plant. In a tapestry-producing factory, white-haired designers and young apprentices alike reported similar politically inspired insomnia ("Revolutionary Tapestries Loved by the Millions," 1968:32).

The eagerness for Mao regalia was endless, and the purity

of the peoples' motivations was explained in no uncertain terms: "This eager demand for the shining Chairman Mao badges is an expression of the increasing depth with which Mao Zedong's thought has taken root in the hearts of the world's people as the great proletarian cultural revolution in China continues its victorious march" ("World's People Eagerly Seek Chairman Mao Badges," 1968:2).

Badges came to be categorized as staples, taking precedence over the daily necessities of life. For example, Zhou (1993) recalls an incident in which a food-processing plant requested emergency assistance during a power shortage. The power supply bureau responded that, in accordance with the instructions of higher administrative offices, badge factories received first priority. The power bureau official then questioned the plant manager. Which is more important, badges or rice? The manager had no response.

According to Zhou (1993), the Shaoshan Mao Badge Factory (now the Shaoshan Arts and Crafts Factory) produced the greatest quantity and variety of badges. The factory usually printed "from where the sun rises," or "visiting Chairman Mao's old residence," with "souvenir from Shaoshan" on the back of its badges. It received the highest-quality manufacturing equipment from the northeastern industrial city of Shenyang and solicited technicians and artists from all over China. At its height, the factory had fixed assets equaling four million yuan and over four hundred designers and technicians. When someone was selected to work at Shaoshan Mao badge factory, the person was given a ceremonial departure by his or her current coworkers, complete with a large, elegant automobile for the trip to Shaoshan (Zhou 1993).

Before the Cultural Revolution, the government had centralized most of the manufacture of badges. This changed during the revolution, when everyone was allowed to produce, distribute, and consume the badges. The government continued to produce badges as well, but did not direct their manufacture or marketing. Badge production did not require official permits. Individuals borrowed and traded molds of Mao's profile, creating their own homemade versions. Designers and manufacturers included the PLA, Red Guard units and rebel organizations, arts and crafts factories, government offices, schools, mines, businesses, blacksmiths, hardware operations, work units, and individuals. Zhou (1993) estimates that at least twenty thousand different organizations produced badges.

With the decentralization of production, badges became more and more accessible to the general population. One collector explains the manner by which a person could obtain badges during the Cultural Revolution:

> There were principally three means by which one could acquire the Mao badge. First, the work unit or the organization to which the person was attached would freely issue their members with badges. Second, individuals could purchase badges themselves. The price paid was usually somewhere between twenty and forty cents and they would usually be bought from the work unit propaganda department. Sometimes shops would also offer a supply. Finally, people would exchange badges among themselves. Many people became avid collectors and went through relatives and friends to collect and exchange badges other than those from their own work unit, province or city. (Dutton 1998:249)

Unlike earlier badges that were confined to the lapels of revolutionary heroes, the masses appropriated badges with little restriction. The historical connection between heroism and Mao badges presented official propagandists with a reliable reference point to market badges. Historically designed for commemoration of revolutionary martyrs and heroes, badges were held in high regard by the people. At the beginning of the Cultural Revolution, the CCP ceremoniously pinned People's Liberation Army soldiers with Mao badges. Early Cultural Revolution propaganda capitalized on the association between badges and martyrdom. Zhou (1993), for example, relates two stories of the commemoration of revolutionary heroics through Mao badges. In the first, a PLA soldier was hospitalized in 1966 for head injuries sustained in a three-year-old battle with Guomindang submarines. A group of Red Guards from Tianjin brought the soldier a bag of Mao badges. The hero, in exchange, gave the Red Guard his own Mao badge as a gift.

In another episode in 1967, PLA soldiers escorted Red Guards to their village via boat when a storm broke out. Passengers fell into the water. The soldiers allegedly saved more than fifty passengers and received Mao badges for their heroism. During the honors, the parents of one of the casualties, a soldier, were introduced. The audience took turns pinning their own Mao badges on the parents, completely decorating them with badges of all sizes and designs.

Cultural Revolution badges adopted an explicitly political tone. Unlike previously made badges that merely commemorated important events, Cultural Revolution badges displayed infinite meanings and came in various shapes and colors. Most were circular, but oval-shaped, flag-shaped, rectangular, and heart-shaped badges were not uncommon. They also differed from earlier badges in the materials used. Due to the sheer numbers of badges created during the Cultural Revolution, badges were made primarily from aluminum, porcelain, and plastic. Rarer badges reflected a more exotic repertoire of materials, including gold, silver, copper, tin, Plexiglas, stone, glass, wood, bamboo, bone, and iron. Estimates suggest that somewhere between three and five billion badges were produced during the Cultural Revolution, representing one hundred thousand different themes (Zhou 1993).

In Cultural Revolution badges, Mao's bright portrait covered the center of the badge, raised above the background. Most aluminum badges used red as the background, and porcelain badges used white. Manufacturers embellished their wares with carved or painted characters and designs surrounding Mao's image and on the back. They produced single, pair, and series badges. Pair badges referred to two badges produced in sequence by the same manufacturer; series badges included multiple badges produced in sequence by the same manufacturer. While sequential badges often offered a unifying theme, they also included a variety of unrelated images, their unity identified by a particular style.

Badges typically were of two colors, the more uncommon ones had three and four, and the quite rare ones five or more. Appropriate colors included red, blue, yellow, green, and white. Portraits of Mao reflected a variety of poses in his youth, middle years, and older ages—often on the same badge. Chinese characters frequently appeared on the front and backs, most commonly expressing admiration of and good wishes for Mao's revolutionary life, in simplified Han characters.

By 1969, the CCP had ordered badge production to cease. It had become a problem for the Chinese government as early as 1967, when design and production of Red Guard armbands and badges were ceased. The decree, citing Mao's philosophy of simplicity as its rationale, suggested that any unnecessary badge production should end:

Recently the consumption of cloth, particularly red cloth, by public organizations has increased enormously. Much of the cloth has been wasted. To further implement our great leader Chairman Mao's call "practice economy while making revolution," the State Council has this proposal to make to Red Guard organizations and other revolutionary mass organizations all over the country: armbands which are now in use must not be changed if they need not be changed; if new ones are really needed, armbands and badges of a smaller size should be adopted, as was the practice during the period of revolutionary civil wars. Cloth for making flags and for other uses must be economized as much as possible, and waste must be strictly prohibited.

While the government expressed concern that the exaggerated Mao badge phenomenon was contrary to Communist dogma on excess, the issue of waste regarding badges took on more practical dimensions as well: the country was running out of aluminum, the primary material used to make badges. Many aluminum factories went bankrupt, and a shortage of aluminum products ensued.

By 1969, Mao announced more stringent sanctions in his famous proclamation: "Give me back my airplanes. It would be far more useful . . . to make airplanes to protect the nation out of the metal being expended in the production of Mao badges" (Barmé 1996:40).

The Central Committee affirmed the inappropriateness of badge collection and trade with a 1969 decree that forbade street exchanges of Mao badges. Mao himself showed discomfort with the immoderate consumption of his image, best exemplified by the collection activities of Lin Biao's wife, Ye Qun. Ye Qun, an avid Mao badge collector, wandered the street markets incognito, accompanied by bodyguards. She proposed trades aggressively, negotiating until she got the badges she wanted. Mao disapproved of her collection and forbade her to present the extravagant collection to him on his seventy-third birthday (Li 1993; Zhou 1993).

Collectors estimate that only one percent of all available badges were made in 1970, and virtually no more badges were made again until Mao's death in 1976, when a brief revival of Mao badges occurred. Only about ten different kinds of badges made directly after Mao's death exist today, typically representing two categories: badges with Mao's portrait surrounded by mourners, proclaiming "Our great leader and tutor, Chairman Mao Zedong, will be immortal"; and badges produced and designed in commemoration of the construction of the Chairman Mao Memorial Hall.

By the end of the Cultural Revolution, the government ordered all citizens to turn in their Mao badges to higher authorities, who would take them to recycling centers. Local authorities targeted known collectors. Still, many insubordinate collectors saved their badges. One collector remembers being allowed to keep his badges after pleading the historical significance of his collecting activity to local cadres. Another remembers: "I, myself, turned in five kilograms of badges. Of course, I picked the ones I didn't like or were not of very good qualities. My leaders at the workplace knew I collected Mao badges, so they talked with me, but I told them that I wouldn't give them all the badges I had."

Ironically, garbage collectors salvaged many of the badges by starting their own collections from the discarded badges. Some of the famous badge collectors in China today confess to buying badges from garbage collectors during this time. Zhou (1993) tells of one collector who befriended garbage collectors solely to buy badges, paying a price slightly higher than the payment for scrap metal.

The existence of massive numbers of Cultural Revolution

Mao badges in contemporary China is due in large part to those Chinese who not only avidly collected badges during the Cultural Revolution but who managed to retain their collections following it. This strategic retention involved circumventing government recalls of badges during the Cultural Revolution and timing the unveiling of unsanctioned collections to the national and international public.

In his discussion of collecting badges, Zhou illustrates what Weiner (1992) refers to as the heroics of "keeping":

> I happened to be visiting my parents for summer vacation when the new [recycling] policy was made. My father, who suffered a lot during the Cultural Revolution, ordered me to turn in all of my collection. For several days I lost sleep and appetite and counted my collection time and again when everybody was asleep at midnight. During this time, I remembered the history of every badge, and behind every badge there was a story. Counting the thousand badges, I had a heavy heart. However, the central government's instructions had to be carried out. Besides, my father's worried and anxious eyes also made me hesitate. After many talks, I eventually decided to adopt a happy middle path and secretly kept five hundred of the most delicate badges. After such a heavy blow, I was depressed for many days. . . . These badges not only bear a period of history, they also bear some very deep emotions. All kinds of cultural relics were left behind by ancient Chinese. Mao Zedong badges are very similar to these cultural relics. . . . If we let these badges disappear totally, it is going to be a great regret to history and a huge disgrace to our future generations. It was these thoughts that made me engage in my old profession again behind my

parents' backs. . . . In order to realize my ambitions, I paid a high price. It became more and more difficult to collect badges after recycling. Psychological pressure for badge collectors was worse too. When I asked for badges, people would ask, "Why do you want a badge?" All I could say was "for fun." In turn, I always got a scolding. "Are badges for fun?" Some people thought I had gone crazy. Some kind-hearted teachers, friends, and elderly people asked me to think before I leap and told me some examples of the unpredictability of political campaigns. (Zhou 1993)

Zhou continues to discuss his personal fallout for his post-recall collecting in a rich anecdote about love and marriage:

One summer night full of stars, I was walking on campus with my girlfriend. As we walked, my eyes were caught by a shining little round object in the grass along the roadside. I dashed over and picked it up. It was a Mao Zedong badge. Wiping off the mud on the badge with my shirt, I held it in my hands and was very excited. By the time I turned around, my girlfriend was long gone. Later, she said, "It is either the badges or me." It was probably because I was stinky and went through other people's garbage. Maybe she felt that being in my company was like being in the company of a tiger and felt anxious that one day she would get into trouble with me. After a lot of painful thought, I chose badges. Later on, some people laughed at me. "You lost a beauty for a piece of badge." I suffered for a long time from the loss of my girlfriend. By the time my colleague introduced a girl from a factory to me, I was almost cynical. The first time we met, I told her of my hobby and possible consequences. "If you agree,

we can carry on; otherwise, there is no more relationship out of it." I was not expecting that this girl would
be interested, but she said enthusiastically, "It is ex-
citing that you enjoy collecting so much. People cannot survive without any pursuit. I also have a big box
of badges. Come, I will show you when you come to
visit." Our shared hobby united our hearts. She gave
me more than four hundred pieces of very delicate
badges as a special gift of love. Many of these badges
filled in the blanks in my collection. So it turned out
to be a blessing in disguise, and I met the love of my
life because of badges. Just as our love was ripening
and right before we were going to have our wedding
ceremony, I was admitted to an arts department at a
university. She waited for me for three years. During
this time, besides my studies, I indulged in badges during most of my spare time, holidays, and weekends. I
went to factories, government offices, and schools to
study ways of making badges, to research quantities
and to collect material. I also visited classmates, colleagues, friends, relatives, and even recycling centers,
for help in locating badges. . . . I graduated in 1987 and
returned to teach. My girlfriend and I got married. Our
married life, though full of hard times, had been very
sweet. In the fall of 1988, I learned that a friend in
Shanghai owned a 1953 silver badge made by Shanghai gold and silver ornament store. I immediately wrote
to him. He wanted to charge me eighty yuan. Although
that is not a lot of money, I was only a teacher whose
salary is very low. At the time, my daughter was just
born and we were very short of money. However, I had
always wanted this badge. . . . I got very restless at
home. My wife was worried. She said, "I see how anxious you are; why don't you go ahead and get it." She

borrowed eighty yuan and mailed it to Shanghai, then took the bus to her parents one hundred li away to borrow eighty yuan to repay the debt. A half a month later I got the badge in the mail, filled with gratitude for my wife. (Zhou 1993)

3

An

Iconography

of Mao

Badges

Cultural Revolution badges were a propaganda medium used by Maoists that the Chinese people swiftly and resolutely decentralized. Though the first badges produced during the Cultural Revolution were markedly generic, the almost immediate decentralization of badge production invited a textual odyssey that makes categorization difficult. Identification of the time, place, and people involved in production present complexities of algebraic proportions when one attempts to historicize even a small fraction of the themes. Production dates and names of manufacturers on badges are spotty. Branches of the People's Liberation Army (PLA) produced badges in large numbers, and they were more apt to identify themselves on badge text than other badges. Homemade badges were rarely labeled. It is also likely that, like many of the publications during the Cultural Revolution, a number of badges were commissioned by central authorities. Thus, I paint badge themes with a broad and speculative stroke and hope that further attempts to historicize badge themes will be made by others in the future.

Authority and Allegiance

The most basic semiotic icon in badges is the color red, *hongse.* According to Chuang (1967), *hong* is an "indispensable verbal icon" connoting the character of Chinese communism as well as one's commitment to Communist ideology. During the Cultural Revolution, hong, a mainstay metaphor for prosperity in the Chinese vocabulary, gained meteoric meaning. This can be seen in the elaboration of hong-based metaphors popular during the Cultural Revolution, such as *hongweiping* (Red Guards), *hongxin* (red heart), *hongshu* (red book), and *hongzhi* (red flag).

We were a Red Guard fighting team. At the moment, we were interrogating a suspect who had been "arrested" by her classmates the day before. . . . She was talking nonstop in a shrill voice. "I am Zhang Heihei! My father is Zhang Laohei! My mother is Zhang Dahei! My younger brother is Zhang Xiaohei! We are a black family! Our home is a black den!" . . . *Hei* means black, so the personal names she made up for herself and her family were Black Black, Old Black, Big Black, and Small Black. . . . "She must be a real counter-revolutionary!" I thought. "How dare she call herself Zhang Heihei?" At the time China was engulfed in a turbulent red storm. Everybody was either a Red Guard, a little red soldier, or a red rebel. Chairman Mao was our red Commander-in-Chief. We called ourselves "his little red devils." We read and quoted his little red book. Wore his red buttons on our chests. Red Flags. Red armbands. Red blood. Red hearts. . . . We could not tolerate anyone who was of a different color. Peach was guilty. Yellow was criminal. Black and white were definitely counter-revolutionary! (R. Yang 1997:229)

Ma illustrates the barrage of redness in a bitter hallucinatory daydream during a Spring Festival celebration in the countryside:

The blood red wine was everywhere: the table, the rug, the floor, the air. A red mist, red waves of light, red silhouettes, red everywhere, red red red, emitting a strong fermented odor. Tons of fresh red blood surged toward me, engulfing me. Rivers of fresh red blood flowed to the mountains, flowed through the ravines, covered the fields, inundated the steppes. Where had it come from? Where was it going? The blood of youth, was it worth nothing in the end? (Ma 1995: 365)

Mao badges are predominantly red in color. Most badges include the color red, thereby providing an immediate visual code of allegiance with Mao's thought.

Badges suggest Mao's ultimate authority through his portrayal as the sun. In these badge images, rays emanate from Mao's image, positioned prominently above the foreground on a background of red. Cultural Revolution propaganda emphasized this notion of Mao as the sun. One children's folk song goes like this:

Red little soldiers are so happy
Side by side, they are busy studying
They love to read revolutionary books since young
Red hearts are always facing the red sun.
(L. Chu 1978:26)

Another Red Guard reflects: "I felt at the time our leader was not an ordinary man. Mao Zedong might have been born as a sun god. We even called him the red sun who arose at Shaoshan" (Bennett and Montaperto 1972:96).

While the sun was the perfect metaphor for Mao—all-powerful and everlasting—sunflowers served as a metaphor for the Chinese people. At least one badge makes the relationship between Mao and the people explicit in a quote, elaborated by one Chinese respondent: "The sunflowers (people) always face (learn from) the red sun (Chairman Mao)." Another badge depicts Mao in a typical scene during the Cultural Revolution—on the review stand overlooking Tiananmen Square—yet, in the place of the throng of Red Guards that typically gathered for review, are seven symbolic sunflowers, all leaning toward Mao. The seven sunflowers represent seven hundred million people, the population of China in the 1960s.

Badges also commonly feature three sunflowers representing the "three loyalties" (*sanzhongyu*), including loyalties for Chairman Mao, his thought, and the proletarian revolutionary line. Trains, lanterns, and lighthouses likewise serve as metaphors for Mao's supreme leadership on badges. The character *zhong*, meaning loyalty, commonly decorated badges. A term that has its roots in taking action in the interest of the emperor, citizens used *zhong* during the Cultural Revolution to connote supreme devotion to Mao Zedong and the Communist Party. A common example on badges can be found in the slogan, "Chairman Mao will forever live in our hearts" (*Mao zhuxi yongyuan huo zai women xinzhong*).

Robert Bishop (1989) notes that, unlike other political stances during the Cultural Revolution, Mao's directives and quotations represented the only politically safe space. Badges carried simple, repetitive slogans, the indoctrination of

Mao's thought via revolutionary redundancy. Quotation badges appeared at the beginning of the Cultural Revolution and remained popular throughout badge production. Slogans repeated most often include the infamous "long live Chairman Mao" (*Mao zhuxi wansui*); "struggle against the selfish and repudiate revisionism" (*dou si pixiou*); and "serve the people" (*wei renmin fuwu*).

"Four great" (*sige weida*) badges were immensely popular following Chen Boda's quote at the first Red Guard rally: "The great leader, the great teacher, the great commander, and the great helmsman, long live Chairman Mao" (*weidade lingxiu, weidade daoshi, weidade tongshuai, weidade doushou, Maozhuxi wansui*).

In addition to quotation badges, badges bearing military symbolism, including planes, warships, and Mao in military uniform, reflected Lin Biao's ascendancy as Mao's second-in-command. Lin Biao's quotes are also widespread on badges, including Lin's early promotion of the "four firsts," as well as what Mao described as his "three and eight style" (*sanba zuofeng*). The four firsts included human qualities, political work, ideological work, and lively thought; and the three and eight style summarized Lin's promulgation of three sentences—"resolutely set the correct political direction," "resolutely suffer an unadorned work style," and "maintain a flexible strategy and tactics"—and eight characters standing for unity, concentration, solemnity, and liveliness (*tuanjie, jinzhang, yansu, huopo*). In addition to the parade of Lin's quotes on badges, the fact that the PLA designed numerous badges reflected his growing status. The most striking example of Lin's growing fame can be found in the fleeting phase when badges featuring Lin with Mao were popular. Lin voiced concern over his growing popularity as early as 1967 in a letter to Zhou Enlai:

In the last month, I have been to three performances. I have observed such slogans as "long live Chairman Mao and Vice Commander Lin Biao. . . . . In order to emphasize Chairman Mao's great importance inside the party, outside the party, internationally and domestically and thus, to build absolute authority of Chairman Mao, I suggest to not mention the latter slogan. Only those slogans that emphasize our great leader Chairman Mao are suitable to the needs of the Chinese as well as the needs of other revolutionary people all over the worlds. . . . From now on, please never mention me together with Chairman Mao in any performance, meeting, documents, media or other publicity and propaganda. . . . Please send this letter to county level government offices for them to announce it to the grassroots level organizations and revolutionary people. (Zhou 1993)

Lin's admonition did not result in his removal from propaganda forms (that would come later); however, badge texts diluted Lin's authority, prioritizing Mao, such as, "Learn from Vice Chairman Lin and be loyal to Chairman Mao." However, in at least one (undated) homemade badge, Lin appears without Mao. Though it was not uncommon for Mao to share the spotlight on badges—as in badges with Mao and Zhou Enlai, and Mao among great Communist minds—this dilution of Mao's image is quite different from the wholesale substitution of Mao. While it is arguable that the example of a Lin-only badge represents dissension, there is something inherently defiant in the survival of any Cultural Revolution badge featuring Lin Biao. Following Lin's death, the government called Lin a traitor and ordered a massive removal of his image. Sun-Childers deftly depicts the day the government announced Lin's insurgence and death:

> The party news now blared into the class in mid-broadcast as an outraged, breathless announcer spoke of treachery and betrayal! A traitor and a devil! A vicious plot against Chairman Mao! An enemy of China had crept into the red army as a spy to destroy the precious red mountain! A Guomindang human time bomb was planted in the heart of the communist party to assassinate our beloved Chairman Mao! This was stunning, terrifying blasphemy! Who wanted to betray and kill our great helmsman? The announcer's next words sent lightning bolts through my heart. "Big traitor Lin Biao will be forever cursed by the people! His stinking corpse will rot on the rubbish heap of history! . . . Big traitor Lin Biao's plane was shot down as he fled across the Soviet border! The people's enemy, Lin Biao, is dead!" My ears rang. This was strange, unreal. Lin Biao, a people's hero for forty years, had fought the Guomindang and the Japanese to save our motherland. The party's spokesman for years, his voice was heard more than any party leader except Chairman Mao. Yet all this time he was plotting to destroy the party and kill Chairman Mao! . . . That hour we tore out Lin Biao's introduction to Chairman Mao's little red book. And we passed around our teacher's knife and carved him carefully out of the frontispiece, leaving his blank silhouette standing like a ghost beside Chairman Mao. . . . All pictures of big traitor Lin Biao were taken down and destroyed. In group-photos, big traitor Lin Biao's image was cut or airbrushed out, leaving an empty gap where he had stood with other party members. (Sun-Childers 1995:67)

Other badges infer Mao's authority by marketing the varied forms of his thought. As a result of Lin's efforts, Mao's writings were not only compulsory reading during the Cultural Revolution, but they came to represent the only intellectual forum. Books that strayed from Mao's philosophy were destroyed. Both Mao's *Quotations* and *Selected Readings* were popular fodder for badge themes, designed in the shape of the books themselves with titles in Chinese and other languages (like the books themselves). The old three articles were another popular badge theme, representing three model writings, including Mao's speech in 1944, "Serve the People," an article written in memory of Norman Bethune in 1939, and an allegorical speech at the Seventh National Congress in 1945, "The Foolish Old Man Who Moved the Mountains."

Badges also imply global repercussions of Mao Zedong thought, depicting Little Red Books revolving around the earth and people around the globe holding up the book. One badge frames Mao's writing in a global context, showing three hands of different colors—white, silver, and black—uplifting the Little Red Book. The back reads, "Asian, African and Latin American revolutionary people love Chairman Mao."

Using the Past to Serve the Present

Symbolic associations with the past are also common on Mao badges. Early Mao badges introduced the novelty of the Cultural Revolution vis-à-vis traditional cultural symbols, such as the palace lantern, a symbol of prosperity. Early badges also pictured pine, evergreen, and cypress trees, all historical symbols of longevity. In a brief discussion of traditional symbols, Li (1993) offers an interesting anecdote that can be related to badges with pines. According to Li, both pine and willow trees were favored in China's folk-loric tradition for their noble and strong-willed character. Mao, debating the two metaphorical trees, the pine and willow, reasoned that pine trees grow fast and strong; despite storm and wind, they stand firmly. Willow trees are adaptable; wherever planted, they grow well, yielding easily to the wind. According to Mao, party members should have both the principle of a pine and the flexibility of a willow. Interestingly, willow trees are conspicuously absent in Mao badges; principle ruled.

Invocation of the prerevolutionary past poses a striking irony in light of the Cultural Revolution campaign to destroy the four olds. Most of these images exist on the very early badges, most likely authorized by Maoists to ensure a higher level of comfort in introducing the novelty of the Cultural Revolution alliance with familiar, often emotionally laden symbols of the past—guilt, or glory, by association.

Later badges recalled the recent revolutionary past. Badges served as a fundamental forum for revolutionary education, imprinted with a visual history of Mao Zedong's life and the life of the Chinese Communist Party. By tracing Chinese history, Mao badges were visual historical texts at a time when correct political knowledge was a priority. By detailing Communist history, badges provided a critical revolutionary education during the Cultural Revolution. A site with enormous appeal was Shaoshan, the rural village of Mao Zedong's birth on December 26, 1893. The most common theme of Mao's childhood on Cultural Revolution badges was his courtyard home, situated on a good-sized farm of several acres surrounded by trees. Shaoshan badges often depict a rising sun over Mao's home, a symbolic rendering of the origins of communism. Memories of Communist "liberation" are also common on badges. For example, badges detail the two-story building that housed the Zunyi conference where Mao became the de facto leader of the CCP. Revolutionary badges also depict the Jinggang Mountains, where pressure from the Guomindang led the Red Army to flee on what turned out to be the Long March, a legendary, winding, 6,000–mile trek. Badges represent in stunning detail the rugged landscape canvassed by Long March revolutionaries, including the snowy mountains, the swampy grasslands, and, most dramatically, the Luding Bridge. The Luding Bridge crossing the Dadu River represented the defining moment of the Red Army's defeat of the Guomindang. Exhausted from the trials of the Long March, the army crossed the chain-link bridge under heavy gunfire to reach victory. Snow's dramatic retelling communicates the intensity of the battle:

> The bridge was built centuries ago, and in the manner of all bridges of the deep rivers of western China. Sixteen heavy iron chains, with a span of some one hundred yards or more, were stretched across the river . . . thick boards lashed over the chains made the road of the bridge, but upon their arrival the reds found that half this wooden flooring had been removed, and before them only the bare iron chains swung to a point midway in the stream. . . . Who would have thought the reds would insanely try to cross on the chains alone? But that was what they did. No time was to be lost. The bridge must be captured before enemy reinforcements arrived. Once more volunteers were called for. One by one red soldiers stepped forward to risk their lives, and, of those who offered themselves, thirty were chosen. Hand grenades and mausers were strapped to their backs, and soon they were swinging out above the boiling river, moving hand over hand, clinging to the iron chains. Red machine guns barked at enemy

redoubts and spattered the bridgehead with bullets. The enemy replied with machine-gunning of his own, and snipers shot at reds tossing high above the water, working slowly toward them. The first warrior was hit, and dropped into the current below; a second fell, and then a third. But as others drew nearer the center, the bridge flooring somewhat protected these dare-to-dies, and most of the enemy bullets glanced off, or ended in the cliffs on the opposite bank. Probably never before had the Szechuanese seen fighters like these—men for whom soldiering was not just a rice bowl, and youths ready to commit suicide to win. . . . At last one red crawled up over the bridge flooring, uncapped a grenade, and tossed it with perfect aim into the enemy redoubt. Nationalist officers ordered the rest of the planking torn up. It was already too late. (Snow 1973: 198)

Dadu River badges evoke the feverish battle almost as dramatically as Snow, detailing the chain links of the bridge, the raging river, the gunfire exchange, and the heroic Communist soldiers falling into the river. Badges further depict Yenan, often showing the caves that sheltered the Communists as the party established itself.

Chan (1985) describes the significance of the theme of death in tales of revolutionary heroism in the socialization of Red Guards. According to Chan, minimizing the tragedy of death effectively diminished the value of life. Particularly when framed in terms of revolutionary heroism, death lost its shock value. Such images worked to subsume notions of individual will with ideals of the collective spirit. Messages of death-defying revolutionary heroism decorated badges, serving both as socialization as well as a supreme political pledge.

Jiang Qing's renovation of the Peking Opera during the Cultural Revolution represented the most insidious illustration of the appropriation of heroic revolutionary images to propagate Cultural Revolution ideals. Revolutionary opera badges represented the dramatic artistic transformations under the leadership of Jiang Qing, whose personal vendettas resulting from her less than successful past as an actress confused her political agenda. Citing her frustration with the feudal themes of the Peking Opera, Jiang whittled the entertainment world down to eight model plays, the only acceptable theater during the Cultural Revolution. These plays included *The Red Lantern*, a story about a railway man and his family who resist Japanese occupation of Northeast China through underground and guerrilla activity; and *The Red Detachment of Women*, a story about a group of revolutionary peasant women on Hainan Island resisting the Guomindang. One scholar's comments on the new imagery in these plays can be read visually on the badges as well: the casual dismissal of the old, symbolized by the introduction of the piano into Peking Opera, replaced by the "new heroes": guerrilla women dancing *en pointe* with rifles (J. Chen 1975). The elegantly crafted display of the model operas on Mao badges diluted the extremes of Jiang's proposed cultural changes by summoning the colorful and dramatic opera tradition in China.

Even couched in socialist realist stylistics, badge graphics represent an ironic link to prerevolutionary history. Andrews (1994) argues that, in addition to adopting traditional archetypes, Cultural Revolution imagery depended on pre–Cultural Revolution stylistic devices. She explains this phenomenon as the result of the inherent contradiction in the desire to perfect the reproduction of revolutionary images without the necessary expertise of the classically trained artists who were persecuted during the Cultural

Revolution. According to Andrews (1994), the strict demands of the socialist-realist style necessitated the very skills that were denigrated during the Cultural Revolution. In response to this problem, "painting correction groups" were formed in which untrained peasants produced images that were "polished" by professionally trained artists who were often temporarily released from labor camps to "collaborate" (Andrews 1994). As a result, the finished products were reminiscent of classic Chinese art.

The perpetuation of Mao's calligraphy during the Cultural Revolution represents the most intriguing and paradoxical presentation of the past. At the same time that Red Guards targeted calligraphic traditions as feudal, they engaged in their own "calligraphic warfare" via big-character posters (Kraus 1991). Red Guards emulated Mao's calligraphy and invoked his poetry on badges. Mao's calligraphy suggested his stamp of approval of Red Guards and became a venue by which a Red Guard could heighten his or her own status by association.

Miners and Mangoes: The Graphic Rise and Fall of the Red Guards

At the beginning of the Cultural Revolution, badge imagery authenticated Red Guard passion. Among the earliest badges are images of Mao reviewing Red Guards, his arm raised in salute to the Red Guards below. Mao bolstered the image of his allegiance with the guards when he wore the armband presented to him at the first Red Guard rally and when he wrote his own big-character poster. The red armband is conspicuously included in badge text, as is the act of Mao writing his big-character poster. The latter badges offer painstaking detail, including his poised brush and the outline of characters on the poster. In both cases, badge imagery rationalized Red Guard action with the reassurance that Mao himself was making a revolution. The visual display of Mao's own participation in Cultural Revolution movements both sanctified and provoked rebellion among Red Guards.

Meisner (1977) has noted that by mid-1968, efforts were made to diffuse the Red Guard movement by propagating models of revolutionary icons. Revolutionary imagery provided Mao and official propagandists a fundamental tool to redirect the volatile Red Guard–driven timbre of the Cultural Revolution to a more mellow tone of revolutionary education. No better example exists than the promotion of the oil painting, *Chairman Mao Goes to Anyuan*, commissioned for an October 1967 exhibit, "Mao Zedong's Thought Illuminates the Anyuan Worker's Movement" (*Mao Zedong sixiang guanghui zhaoliang Anyuan gongren geming yundong*) at the Museum of Revolutionary History. The Cultural Revolution Small Group organized the exhibit to assail Liu Shaoqi; Mao's wife instructed painters to supplant Liu's image with Mao's, thereby undermining Liu's leadership in the organization of the famous 1922 coal miner's strike in Anyuan:

> The radiant, youthful Mao Zedong stands contemplatively on a mountain path, looking as though his destination was St. Peter's Pearly Gates rather than a coal mine. Indeed, the classically schooled artist claims to have taken his inspiration from a Raphael Madonna. The practical business of revising the standard historical account by replacing Liu Shaoqi with Mao Zedong as the mastermind of the famous strike might present difficulties even if the young artist believed, as he did, in the ideological accuracy of the newly simplified history. This work avoids concrete problems concerning

who did what when by severing the genre of history painting from its mundane ties to an identifiable physical setting. It doesn't matter where Mao is or what he is doing, for the transcendent nobility of his cause and character are clear. (Andrews 1994:339)

As interesting as the compilation of the Anyuan painting itself is the government-inspired propagation of the image as a model for the Cultural Revolution in 1968. Following Jiang Qing's blessing of the Anyuan image, an intensive propaganda campaign began. Andrews (1994) notes that officials celebrated the *People's Daily* reproduction of the image with parades and festivals, complete with dancers circling the reproductions. Such efforts resulted in a massive reproduction of the image, an estimated nine hundred million copies printed by the end of the Cultural Revolution.

Mao's effort to gain control over the growing violence between Red Guard factions propelled the marketing of the Anyuan image. On July 3, 1968, the party issued a notice demanding the dismantling of barricades, return of seized weapons, and immediate cessation of violence and disruptions to travel and communications (Yan and Gao 1996).

Officials strategically cultivated the Anyuan image to moderate Red Guard and rebel violence by presenting a diversionary image of revolutionary spirit. The Anyuan image held the additional semiotic advantage of Mao's youth; in his early twenties during the Party's work in Anyuan, Mao closely paralleled the youthful Red Guards. Instead of radical violence and fear, however, young Mao projected an aura of courage, hope, trust, leadership, and heroism, as well as selfless service to rural communities. Following the directive, publicity surrounding the Anyuan painting peaked to a near hysterical level. The words of painter Liu Chunhua were canned and packaged:

What workers, peasants, soldiers and Red Guards in their hundreds of millions keenly want is for brushes and paint to be used to portray the noble image of our great leader Chairman Mao, and paintings be used to disseminate Mao Zedong's thought and sing the praises of Chairman Mao's revolutionary line. We revolutionary artists regard this as our fundamental and most glorious task. Chairman Mao received Red Guards on many occasions during the unprecedented Great Proletarian Cultural Revolution. The sight of his tall figure and kindly face, and of him smiling and waving his hand to us thrilled me. I shouted at the top of my voice, "Long live Chairman Mao! A long, long life to him!" On those occasions I had a great desire to paint a picture of him. . . . We visited the Anyuan coal mine where Chairman Mao lit the flames of revolution. The most essential thing in creating the painting was to present the brilliant image and great thought of our great leader Chairman Mao during his youth. We had an extensive collection of articles and poems written by Chairman Mao in his youth, reminiscences of his revolutionary activities and historical data about Anyuan. We placed Chairman Mao in the forefront of the painting, advancing toward us like a rising sun bringing hope to the people. . . . Through meaningful details, we tried to bring out the significance of Chairman Mao's action: his head held high in the act of surveying the scene before him conveys his revolutionary spirit, dauntless before danger and violence, courageous in struggle, and daring to win. His clenched fist depicts his revolutionary will, fearless of all sacrifice and determined to surmount every difficulty to emancipate China and mankind, and shows his confidence in victory. The old umbrella under his right arm shows his hard-working style of traveling in all weather over great distances, across mountains and rivers, for the revolutionary cause. Striding firmly over rugged terrain, Chairman Mao is seen blazing the trail for us, breaking through obstacles in the way of our advance and leading us forward to victory. The hair grown long in a very busy life is blown by the autumn wind. His long plain gown, fluttering in the wind, is a harbinger of the approaching revolutionary storm. The sun is rising, touching the Anyuan hills with red. With the arrival of our great leader, blue skies appear over Anyuan. The hills, sky, trees, and clouds are means used to evoke artistically the great image of the red sun in our hearts. The clouds are depicted as Chairman Mao describes in a poem—"riotous clouds drift past, swift and tranquil." They indicate that Chairman Mao is arriving in Anyuan at a moment of sharp class struggle and show in contrast how tranquil, confident, and firm Chairman Mao is at that moment. They also portend the new storm of class struggle that will soon begin. In creating this work we felt that the portrayal of Chairman Mao's facial expression was the most difficult and essential thing. The key to solving this problem is to grasp Mao Zedong's thought and use it as a guide. We became convinced that we should strive for an expression of revolutionary farsightedness and heroism of Chairman Mao. We would show Chairman Mao's great determination to wholeheartedly serve the emancipation of China and mankind and reflect his unswerving revolutionary spirit, fearing neither danger nor obstacles. In short, we would show that the red sun in our hearts is the most talented, outstanding and brilliant leader among those who emerge only once in hundreds of years in the history of the world and once in several thousand years in China. . . . In our mind's eye we seemed to see the Anyuan miners in the '20s under the threefold oppression of imperialism, feudalism, and bureaucratic capitalism in an abyss of suffering, filled with wrath, and longing for the early arrival of the great leader. A red sun suddenly broke through the dark clouds over the Anyuan hills. . . . With boundless love for Chairman Mao and burning hatred for China's Khrushchev (Liu Shaoqi), we did this oil painting. We felt we were not just wielding our brushes but were fighting in defense of Chairman Mao and his revolutionary line. ("Painting Pictures of Chairman Mao Is Our Greatest Happiness," 1968)

The Anyuan movement was a subtle hint to Red Guards and rebel organizations to stop the violence. By the end of July 1968, the party enacted its directions to cease violence more dramatically, and, here again, badges played a role in disseminating the message. According to Yan and Gao (1996), Red Guards at Qinghua University were manufacturing their own weapons, including rifles, hand grenades, spears, tanks, and bullets. As a more ardent response, Mao sent "workers' propaganda teams," backed by the PLA, to the country's schools and universities to reestablish order. One of the most climactic episodes centered on the July 26 dispatch of 30,000 workers and PLA soldiers to Qinghua University to intervene in factional fighting among Red Guards who disregarded Mao's order to lay down arms. Violence ensued, resulting in a handful of deaths and hundreds of injuries. On August 5, Mao presented the workers' propaganda team with a gift of mangoes given to him by the foreign minister of Pakistan. The message vis-à-vis the mangoes was clear: Mao's loyalty was now with the workers who would go to whatever lengths necessary to end the factional fighting among students. The distribution of mangoes was a prime example of Mao's strategy of symbolic support. Where he once took up pen and paper to write a big-character poster and donned an armband and Mao badge to support student Red Guards, in 1968, Mao signaled his support of the workers with a gift of mangoes.

Officials fervently propagandized the gift of mangoes, as well as the purported reception of the gift, as in the following article:

> Our great teacher and great leader Chairman Mao on August 5 sent mangoes, a treasured gift he had received from foreign friends, to the worker-peasant Mao Zedong thought propaganda team in the Chinese capital. . . . As the joyous news spread, the Qinghua campus was a scene of jubilation. Cheers of "a long, long life to Chairman Mao!" rang out to the skies. The revolutionary fighters of the team declared excitedly: "Our great leader Chairman Mao's heart is always linked with ours. We are determined to hold the great red banner of Mao Zedong's thought still higher and be boundlessly loyal to the great leader Chairman Mao. Rallying closely around the proletarian headquarters with Chairman Mao as the leader and vice-chairman Lin Biao as the deputy leader, we will have a unified will, coordinate our steps and actions at the command of the proletarian headquarters and firmly carry out Chairman Mao's latest instructions. We are determined to criticize and repudiate the reactionary theory of 'many centers,' promptly see through and smash the schemes and plots of the handful of class enemies in their vain attempt to undermine Chairman Mao's proletarian headquarters, and win all-round victory in the great proletarian cultural revolution. ("Basket of Fruit," 1968)

In typical officialese, the same article captured the enthusiastic response of the very same Red Guards who fell victim to the team:

> Young revolutionary Red Guard fighters and revolutionary teachers, students and staff of Qinghua University were overjoyed at this happy event. Many young Red Guard fighters declared excitedly: "This joyous event is also the greatest inspiration, greatest education and greatest encouragement given us by Chairman Mao. We love what Chairman Mao loves, and support what he supports. We are determined firmly to support the revolutionary actions of the propaganda team. We will closely unite under the wise leadership of the proletarian headquarters with Chairman Mao as the leader and Vice-Chairman Lin Biao as the deputy leader, follow closely Chairman Mao's great strategic plan, implement his latest instructions in a prompt, all-round way, strengthen our unity against the enemy, direct the spearhead of struggle squarely against China's Khrushchev and the handful of enemy agents, renegades and diehard capitalist roaders, do a good job in struggle-criticism-transformation in our university and carry through to the end the great proletarian cultural revolution in Qinghua University!" ("Basket of Fruit," 1968)

In one of the more puzzling propaganda twists, the mangoes took on lives of their own, purportedly waxed for preservation, models of which were zealously reproduced. Mao's private physician described the fate of the mangoes that made their way to the Beijing Textile Factory where he lived at the time:

> The workers at the factory held a huge ceremony, rich in the recitation of Mao's words, to welcome the arrival

of the mango, then sealed the fruit in wax, hoping to preserve it for posterity. The mangoes became sacred relics, objects of veneration. The wax-covered fruit was placed on an altar in the factory auditorium, and workers lined up to file past it, solemnly bowing as they walked by. No one had thought to sterilize the mango before sealing it, however, and after a few days on display, it began to show signs of rot. The revolutionary committee of the factory retrieved the rotting mango, peeled it, then boiled the flesh in a huge pot of water. Another ceremony was held, equally solemn. Mao again was greatly venerated, and the gift of the mango was lauded as evidence of the Chairman's deep concern for the workers. Then everyone in the factory filed by and each worker drank a spoonful of the water in which the sacred mango had been boiled. After that, the revolutionary committee ordered a wax model of the original mango. The replica was duly made and placed on the altar to replace the real fruit, and workers continued to file by, their veneration for the sacred object in no apparent way diminished. (Li 1994:503)

In similar mango lore, a Beijing printing plant received one of the mangoes and held a rally in its honor. After the rally, the workers were "frantic" to preserve the mango for future generations. After an exhaustive search for an appropriate chemical treatment, workers injected the mango and worked through the night to build a glass case for it. Sun-Childers (1995) claims that the masses placed mangoes beneath Mao's picture, offering him bites to reflect their hospitable loyalty.

Like the Anyuan image, mangoes became legendary on Mao badges, linked with slogans used by the workers. Mangoes were also a staple design for badges commemorating the establishment of "revolutionary committees," the authority that had superseded the Red Guards across China to restore normalcy. Badges typically featured a single mango or a platter of mangoes below the omnipresent Mao profile.

Mao advertised the new revolutionary committees as a combination of cadres, the army, and the masses, working together to practice, defend, and promote Mao's instruction. The popularity of both Anyuan and mango badges was a particularly compelling example of the Communist propaganda machine. The PLA issued these badges in large numbers to communicate the dissolution of Red Guard supremacy and the new direction of the Cultural Revolution. Given the popularity of badges among Red Guards, they would have been a powerfully direct medium. However, the revered mangoes must have, indeed, tasted bitter to the Red Guards, who once enjoyed immense power with Mao's support, raising questions about the appropriation of the mango symbol on badges. Particularly given that Red Guards were so involved in the production of badges, one wonders if there is any credence to speculation that the rabid consumption of the mango image reflected the subtle, tongue-in-cheek humor of Chinese underdogs: overdoing a good thing until it reaches a point of absurdity. Certainly, other possibilities abound. There was, undoubtedly, no shortage of citizens exhilarated by the dismissal of the red vanguard who could have easily played a hand in propagandizing mangoes on badges. Red Guards on the fringes of the factional fighting, too, revealed an eagerness to end it. Take, for example, Luo's reaction to the workers' propaganda teams:

> Under the policy of "the working class rules all," instituted in 1968, the squad of the workers' propaganda team of Mao Zedong thought occupied my middle

school. They ordered the warring factions of Red Guards to stop fighting and join together in the "revolutionary union," and they expelled the Red Guards from the Ox Ghost Reeducation Ranch, where many teachers had been confined to perform slave labor. Some teachers were liberated in the process. . . . The working class was now in control; the era of the Red Guards' dominion was over. Most of us welcomed the change. We were growing older but acquiring neither skills nor knowledge. Out of sheer boredom, students had been starting street fights or vandalizing local stores. Those willing to get out of bed only to eat were considered good children, because they stayed out of trouble. (Luo 1990:14)

Mao hailed the establishment of revolutionary committees throughout China as a great victory of the Cultural Revolution: power had been reinstated. Mao badges commemorated the establishment of revolutionary committees ferociously, detailing names, dates, and places of establishment. A phase of "red mountains and red rivers" badges suggested the unified redness of the entire country. In reality, however, the revolutionary committees were fragile and fraught with the legacy of political infighting. While the official line on revolutionary committees revealed none of the factional pandemonium that plagued them, the text of Mao badges hints at nagging dissension over relative minutiae. For example, the common design for revolutionary committee badges was a map of China, with all provinces colored red. According to Zhou (1993), the production of maps on revolutionary committee badges resulted in disagreement regarding the symbolic management of Taiwan. On some of the maps, Taiwan is not shaded red on the basis that Taiwan, indeed, was not "red" and should be distinguished as outside of the mainland national fervor. On others, Taiwan is not distinguished, implying the zealous ambition to "liberate" Taiwan. Ideological debates surrounding map representations flourished to the extent that most producers adopted alternative designs (Zhou 1993).

Soon after declaring mainland China a unified "red" in the fall of 1968, Mao exiled Liu Shaoqi from the Party and revived the rustification program, mandating the removal of disgruntled youth from their urban camps to the countryside. In a corresponding move, Mao rejuvenated May Seventh schools, the rural labor camps where cadres were sent. Mao badges promoted both send-down programs in typical graphic style, featuring Mao in a peasant hat surrounded by wheat.

The Ninth Congress resulted in a wave of new badges replete with celebratory designs of balloons and banners. Ninth Congress badges adopt the stance of unity and closure extolled by the congress, best reflected by the intricately designed series badges. Badges portray Mao speaking with generous detail: his fingers extended to make a point, stars decorating the ceiling, wrinkled curtains behind him. Of course, the manufacture of series badges, in itself, suggested a completed narrative.

Anomalous Badges

The decentralization of the production of Mao badges invites the opportunity to examine badges as an unofficial medium whose construction invited individual expression. Gray (1992), for example, elaborates on the notion of citizen participation in Chinese propaganda with her thesis that public involvement in propaganda loosens controls on what can be said and who can say it. Still, the populist nature of making Cultural Revolution badges cannot be overdrawn; however individualized, replicating Mao was a politically sensitive process. One respondent tells a story of a friend whose homemade rendition of a Mao portrait landed him the label of counter-revolutionary:

> I know a comrade who worked at a propaganda department during the Cultural Revolution. A representative from the military asked him to design a Mao badge. This person came to me, because he knew I had a big collection. He borrowed a couple of my badges and copied the design, leaving the upper part of the draft empty. He put this piece of design paper he made with very detailed and elaborate surroundings but with a big hole in the middle onto a Mao poster on the wall. He was not drawing a Mao portrait; he just did a framework and put it around a Mao poster. He was immediately labeled a counter-revolutionary.

The question of whether or not such creative sprawl might be interpreted as an expression of dissent is particularly complex. Among the wealth of badges that exists today, anomalies are rare. An intriguing example surrounds Communist doctrine on the directions of left and right. During the Cultural Revolution, the emphasis on leftist ideology permeated everyday interactions. The crime of metaphorically looking to the right translated more literally in the production of material culture. Badges almost always feature Mao's left profile. However, a small number of badges with Mao facing right exist today. The Mao-facing-right badges feature Mao's generic profile reversed. This does not include images of Mao facing right that have been borrowed from celebrated photographs in which he is looking to the right, though intrigue surrounds this category as well; producers commonly reversed such images to present Mao in historic pose but facing left. Li (1993) attributes the existence of Mao-facing-right badges to factional alliances, though Zhou (1993) describes such badges as mistakes that resulted in tragic consequences for the producers. The attention given to such badges by scholars as well as the improbability of such repetitive mistakes in an environment that left little doubt for correct protocol hints at the possibility of subversive potential in Mao badges.

Overall, it is unlikely that a person would have taken the political risk of intentionally producing subversive badges. It is even more unlikely that such badges would have survived the excessive monitoring and purging that befell counter-revolutionary crimes during the Cultural Revolution. The subversive potential of anomalous badges lies more in the intrigues that followed the production of defective badges than seditious manufacture. The machinations surrounding anomalous badges are undoubtedly due, in part, to the probability that interpretations were easily confused and distorted in the clamber to align oneself with the correct party line.

As a medium that invited individual expression, Mao badges embodied myriad interpretive possibilities, including dissenting voices. As Mao badges became increasingly popular during the Cultural Revolution, their enthusiastic consumption involved an interpretive richness that far surpassed visual semiotics. While the possibility of dissension in badge text itself cannot be entirely ruled out, the lives of badges extend well beyond their thematic intrigue as they moved among and around citizens working to stay afloat in the red sea of the Cultural Revolution.

4

Bloodlines,

Political

Capital,

and Badges

Beyond their textual content, Mao badges served as a strategic approach accumulating political capital that could effectively shield political impropriety. By consuming Mao badges, Chinese citizens aspired to political virtue to numb the trauma of the Cultural Revolution without risking subservience to its perceived enemies of bourgeois Westernization. Badges served as a currency to attain political capital. The rabid consumption of Mao badges had less to do with a cult mentality than the desperation to authenticate one's redness and, in the case of factional fighting, "out-red" one another.

Bourdieu's notion of "symbolic capital"—those more nebulous status accouterments outside of economic wealth—provides an appropriate framework for analysis of the accrual of political capital vis-à-vis Mao badges. Mao's iconographic career owes its prosperity to the symbolic appropriation of badges by which Red Guards sought to distinguish their political virtue. Beyond Red Guard infighting, political capital was a high priority for all Chinese during the Cultural Revolution. Consumption of Mao icons served as a uniquely accessible and highly desirable way for everyday Chinese to gain the political capital needed to survive during the Cultural Revolution.

Nouveau Red

Red Guards' interpretive ingenuity regarding the correct management of Mao's image (as well as his words and thought) served as a litmus test for red status. By enforcing exacting standards over the management of Mao's image, Red Guards strove to raise their own status as the enviable elite that could access that image. Lackadaisical or careless handling of Mao's images and words resulted in severe consequences under the red terror. Red Guards perfected the art of manufacturing evidence that unveiled counterrevolutionary codes, the more inspired, the more reflective of one's talent for redness. A junior high classroom scene illustrates a typical code-cracking scene:

> Little Bawang pointed to Chairman Mao's portrait at the front of our classroom and exclaimed, "Look! Chairman Mao has only one ear!" Sure enough, the face was turned slightly to the right, showing only the left ear. A few students laughed. "What are you laughing about?" Little Bawang snarled. "This is a serious political problem. Every normal person has two ears, so why did this painter paint Chairman Mao with only one?" The class divided into two schools of thought. Yuling and I and a few others saw the missing ear as a

question of artistic realism. But Little Bawang's view won over a majority. They began discussing whether to report the missing ear to the School Party Committee. (Gao 1987:40)

In a curious parallel with European noblemen, Red Guards appropriated material culture to stake claims to status. At the onset of the Cultural Revolution, loyalist Red Guards donned armbands and badges to signify their exclusive membership. Borrowed from a prestigious history, badges, particularly, served as powerful "weapons of exclusion" (Douglas and Isherwood 1989). Wen notes that "just as the red kerchief of the Young Pioneers was a necessary badge of a Red successor, the armband of the Red Guard was the mark of a good person" (1995:7). Gao describes a Red Guard who shrouded himself in material symbols to intimidate classmates:

> Little Bawang had support from Yuanchao, whose combined revolutionary soldier/poor-peasant lineage made him the reddest Red Guard in our class. "Our parents followed Chairman Mao in making the revolution and liberating China. Only we can go!" he said, standing extra straight so that we could get a good look at his new outfit—his father's baggy old Red Army uniform, cinched with a leather belt. He also had pinned on his chest an enameled badge the size of a one-fen coin that showed Chairman Mao's profile, golden against a red background. (Gao 1987:113)

By adopting the material insignia of armbands and army uniforms, Red Guards poised themselves in the footsteps of their forefathers. Of course, Mao himself went to great lengths to sanctify the authority of the Red Guards through donning the very same signifiers that they adopted. These

Figure 1. Early badge created during the 1950s in support of the War to Resist U.S. Aggression and Aid Korea. It was circulated among soldiers in Korea and Korean citizens.

Figure 2. Badges produced at the beginning of the Cultural Revolution (1966) with traditional images of lanterns, cypress trees, and evergreens, depicting longevity and prosperity.

Figure 3. Porcelain badges, which became somewhat of a political liability due to their fragility—a broken badge invited criticism and persecution.

Figure 4. Mao as the sun-god surrounded by seven symbolic sunflowers representing China's population of seven hundred million people. Bottom badge features the infamous mangoes given by Mao to the military team he directed to quell factional violence among Red Guards in 1968.

Figure 5. Mao as the great helmsman of the Cultural Revolution.

Figure 6. Badges featured the obligatory words and thought of Mao Zedong, including the Three Articles, *Mao's Quotations* (the Little Red Book), and *Mao's Selected Works*. Note the bottom badge is in English, as part of the initiative to globalize Mao's thought. It was produced, however, in spite of the prohibition of English-language study during the Cultural Revolution.

Figure 7. (*left*) Three of the eight model plays endorsed by Mao's wife, Jiang Qing, in place of the feudalistic Peking Opera. From top to bottom: *The White-Haired Girl, The Red Lantern,* and *The Red Detachment of Women.* Visual signs of the new political order include the piano (nonexistent in the Peking Opera) and women dancing *en pointe* with rifles.

Figure 8. (*right*) Samples of badges depicting Mao Zedong's life and revolutionary history, including (top to bottom) the site of the Zunyi conference; the houseboat where the early Communist Party met to escape the Guomindang; and Shaoshan, or "where the sun rises," Mao's birthplace.

Figure 9. Badges illustrating the Long March, the definitive trek by Communists to overtake the Guomindang. The top badge represents a composite of the Long March, including the Zunyi conference, swamplands, snowy mountains, Luding Bridge, and Yenan. The bottom badge offers more graphic detail of the Luding Bridge battle, where Communist soldiers crossed over the chain-link bridge whose planks had been removed by the Guomindang to thwart its enemies.

Figure 10. Mao going to Anyuan—a heavily propagandized image during the Cultural Revolution, posing a youthful, heroic Mao.

Figure 11. Peasant Mao: badges sporting Mao in peasant garb to advertise the rustification movement in which Mao sent students and cadres to the countryside to learn revolution from the peasants. The "57" in the top badge represents Mao's May Seventh schools, designed specifically for cadre reeducation.

Figure 12. A variety of miniature badges featuring Mao's supreme and, in the case of the middle two badges, global leadership. The top badge is unique in its depiction of Mao facing right, a subversive visual statement challenging the Maoist clique.

Figure 13. These badges aptly illustrate the interpretive minefield of the Cultural Revolution. This stance, borrowed from a photograph portraying Mao facing right, was commonly reversed to ensure the correct political direction of left.

Figure 14. A rare home-made badge, featuring Lin Biao by himself. Though Lin was regularly featured with Mao, "Lin only" badges represented a short-lived graphic challenge to Mao's ultimate authority.

毛主席和他的亲密战友
同志检阅文化
革命大军

毛主席万岁

Figure 15. (*above*) After Lin Biao's death, the Mao clique ordered the mass destruction of his image. This statue illustrates the attempt to erase Lin from the public imagination, though the shadow where Lin once stood remains visible.

Figure 16. (*right*) Mao in the line of great Communist minds, including Lenin, Marx, Engels, and Stalin.

Figure 17. China's social architect: one of the Deng Xiaoping badges of the 1980s.

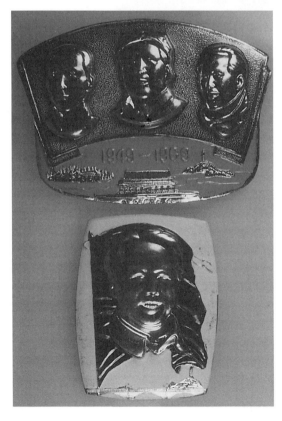

Figure 18. Many faces of Mao: examples of later badges (1969) invested with greater esthetic elegance.

Figure 19. Mao at leisure: more examples of the creativity and playfulness apparent in the later (1969) series of badges.

Figure 20. One of many antique and curio street markets selling Mao badges and other Cultural Revolution relics.

Figure 21. Taxi Mao. This picture illustrates an urban phenomenon where taxi drivers hang Mao's picture in their windows as superstitious buffers against traffic accidents.

Figure 22. A young student on the streets of Beijing donning a small Mao badge on her shirt.

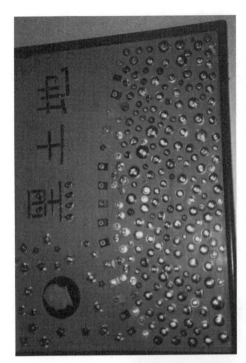

Figure 23. Mao badges decorating the rustic dining room of a Chinese Cultural Revolution theme restaurant in Beijing.

Figure 24. A backpack covered with badges, reminiscent of Chinese youth sent to the countryside during the Cultural Revolution, now serves as decoration for a Cultural Revolution theme restaurant in Beijing.

factors, combined with the Red Guards' immaturity and ingrained sense of entitlement, only bloated their illusion of self-importance and indestructibility.

At the beginning of the Cultural Revolution, it was inconceivable for lower-echelon people of questionable ancestry to threaten the Red Guard hierarchy, and student "out-circles" humbly cowed to Red Guard authority. To falsely assume membership in an unassigned category was unthinkable, and the inhumane treatment by Red Guards effectively squelched their contentious claims to authority. Once emboldened by Mao's shift from the bloodline theory, students of less prestigious backgrounds, or rebel guards, cultivated political participation as proof of political virtue, despite questionable family origins. It is not surprising that the massive production and consumption of Mao badges paralleled the rise of the rebel guards (Zhou 1993; Li 1993). Mao badges presented exceedingly accessible, potent, and fertile ground for the rebel challenge. Badges presented a small, portable, and readily available venue for Mao's image. As historic insignia, badges yielded a significant symbolic weight. As emblems of loyalty to Mao, they were attainable and, therefore, easily appropriated as symbols of political character. One respondent explained: "The discipline and rules among the Red Guards during the Cultural Revolution were more severe than the laws today. The children of the five black categories could not become Red Guards. They could wear Mao badges, though, because that was a way to express love to Chairman Mao. It did not matter if you were black or red."

As objects that were worn, badges carried the dual weight of political statement and political action, an ideal resource for rebel guards. Rebels hungrily appropriated badges to gain retribution and indicate status rearrangements. Gao (1987:135), for example, remembers obtaining a Mao badge during *chuanlian* (the movement of students across the country to "exchange revolutionary experiences") for a friend previously barred from Red Guard participation: "I unpinned Yuling's Chairman Mao badge from the inside of my pocket and looked at it glinting in the day's last light. I had been looking forward to giving Yuling her present and watching her face light up."

In an interesting anecdote, Zhou (1993) describes his fervor for collecting badges as symbolic retribution for harassment endured as a "black" during the Cultural Revolution:

> In 1964, I was only three years old. Held in my parents' arms and out of deep love for Beijing, I followed my parents in military positions to a remote county in Guizhou. I was a first-grader when the Cultural Revolution started. My treasure box was full of different items. The fire of the Cultural Revolution also swept this remote mountainous village. People started to wear Mao Zedong badges of all kinds on their chests. In my heart, these badges represented holiness and beauty. How I wished that I could have these beautiful badges too. However, at the time, my father was labeled a capitalist roader and was criticized every day. My mother had to work in a cafeteria. Neither of them at the time had energy for my little wish. In the spring of 1968, a relative from my hometown came to visit. In front of his chest was a delicate badge. Chairman Mao's profile was made out of phosphorus and shone in the dark. I was very attracted to this very rare, delicate badge. When he left, I followed him for several miles and finally moved him. He took it off his chest and gave it to me. I was so delighted, so excited wearing this very special badge in the little mountain town.

However, before long, one rainy afternoon, I was playing dam building with several of my classmates. Suddenly, a wave of dirty water crushed my dam. "Zhou, give me your red scarf and the badge. As a five black category, you do not deserve to wear these." I looked up and it was a teacher and several little Red Guards. As stubborn a child as I was, I refused to give up and guarded my chest. However, these people "adopted revolutionary action," pushed me down to the ground into the muddy water and robbed my Red Guard scarf and took my badge away. Soaked in mud, I cried and walked home to tell my parents. I was so hurt and sad, but both my parents were not able even to protect themselves. How could they have relieved their child's pain? All they could do was sigh. The only comfort I got was my loving mother's powerful tears. Ever since then I secretly promised to myself that I would collect more Mao Zedong badges than anybody else. With determination, I gradually started my journey of collecting. Sometimes my uncles and aunties came to visit us. I always stared at their badges. They would generously give me one if they had extra. Sometimes I would risk losing face to seek after good new badges worn by friends and relatives. I worked half a day for one badge. I walked several miles to get a badge. I have called others "grandpa" to please him to get a badge. We lived about five li from a local rice station. Every month we had to buy rice and flour several times. It was a big headache for the whole family to carry it back home. Some kind-hearted neighbors would have helped us were it not for the gossip they would face. So my brother and I had to do it. At that time, I was still in grade school. My brother was four years older than me. At the time, he could carry more than thirty jin of rice.

I could only do a bit more than ten jin. Every time we carried these home, my mom gave us five fen to get some candy. Although I did less work, I always got my brother's share so I could use this one jiao to "invite" two little badges, or one big badge, from the Xinhua bookstore. At the same time, I also exchanged badges from my little friends with self-made toys, wood knives, water guns. . . . I hid my precious collection very carefully and never dared to show them off to anybody else. I was only fourteen years old when I graduated from junior high and was forced up the mountain and down the country. . . . I never stopped my collecting of badges during this period. By the time the Cultural Revolution was over, I had already collected several hundred types and over one thousand badges. Most were set badges of top-class unique design. The ten years of chaos ended, and my whole family regained joy. I was admitted to a school in the provincial capital. People started to cool down from the craze and personal superstition and started to suspect and resist the Cultural Revolution. As a special product of this historical era, the Mao Zedong badges had undoubtedly become a historical package. (Zhou 1993)

With such material co-optation, political virtue was no longer the sacred domain of an elite few. Mao badges offered a wealth of semiotic political tools for status emulation that posed a dilemma for loyalists. The rebel challenge, in turn, led cadre's children to "check all of the ways to upward mobility for the lesser classes" (A. Chan 1992:66). McCracken's (1988) image of a "riot of consumption" is an apt description for the proliferation of Mao consumption that ensued as Red Guard factions strove to out-red one another. Rebels were particularly apt to challenge loyalist authority through novelty, fashioning endless techniques to define themselves in "contradistinction" to loyalists (Chan, Rosen, and Unger 1980). It was no longer enough to simply acquire and wear a badge. One's redness depended instead on the novelty with which one could design and/or consume a badge. The result was a fanatical diversification of badge content and use.

Distinction

As symbolically rich textual emblems and pieces of material culture, Mao badges were particularly prolific in efforts toward distinction. The more distinctive the badge, the better; badge size, theme, and material denoted revolutionary vigor. Badge designs were trendy, and Red Guards pursued a variety of designs. New designs imparted greater potentials of redness in that they often reflected regional markings associated with the chuanlian spirit. Clustered in these various sites, students compared collections and traded among themselves. The varied revolutionary sites that drew students manufactured badges reflecting their local claims to fame and, often, presented them with these badges as gifts. Students also offered locals gifts of Mao badges, as in the following story:

> We lost some of our exuberance when we saw the poverty-stricken villagers everywhere. In one place a little boy wanted to trade all the herbal medicine he had gathered that day for my Mao badge. Tears welled up in my eyes. I reckoned it was the deep love of our people for Chairman Mao. I did not accept the herbs of course. No use anyway. I quickly took off my badge, collected several other shapes from my classmates, and gave

them all to the kid. He accepted them as if they were treasures. His mother told him not to play with them but to worship them. In the rural areas people used to hang up a picture of the kitchen god. Now they worshipped Mao's portrait in its place. (Feng 1991:86)

Chuanlian offered students an unprecedented opportunity to visit famous places and travel throughout China. Travel to sites of revolutionary significance enhanced one's revolutionary credentials. Niu-Niu (1995) reiterates the relationship between Mao consumption and revolutionary credentials in her memory of wanting to visit Mao so that her heart would be "bright red." The value in new badge designs related to revolutionary sophistication in that they reflected the most current manifestation of revolutionary esthetics. To obtain the latest badge fashion was to exhibit one's vigilant acumen of revolutionary politics.

Gao, for example, describes the appeal of innovative designs: "We accumulated the newest designs depicting revolutionary landmarks—Chairman Mao's birthplace, Shaoshan, the Jinggang Mountains, where the Communist Party had set up its base after Chiang Kai-shek's massacre in 1927, the Long March, and Yenan, the base area from the end of the Long March to the eve of Liberation (1987:166).

One respondent remembers the enthusiasm for the curious trend of badges labeled as having been made from American aircraft wreckage during the Vietnam War. Zhou (1993) comments that when Mao-as-steersman badges emerged, they were worth at least five smaller badges in Shanghai. At least one respondent offers a similar sentiment: "If I saw a new piece, I would offer them five, or even ten, of mine just to get that one piece that I liked."

Another Red Guard remembers: "A Chinese proverb says, 'Things which are few are also expensive.' Any sort of

Mao badge produced in only small quantities and looking a little different from other ones was immediately recognized as higher in value, so Red Guards who had them would demand higher prices. One such badge could be exchanged for seven or eight, or more, common ones" (see Bennett and Montaperto 1972:99). Gao also hints at worth in a description of an exchange: "One youngster was offering a large golden badge for two small ones. Excitedly, I traded him the two badges I had gotten in Beijing. Now I had a big one as well as the small one Chairman Deng had obtained. Walking among the haggling dealers, I stopped to admire a new design, consisting of a small red badge inlaid on a five-pointed gold star. The owner wanted ten small badges for it, an impossibility for me" (Gao 1987:151).

A sense of urgency in exhibiting the most recent badge production prevails on badges, as evident by inclusion of the date, place, and even the time of production. The combination of innovative badges with other esthetic details such as size, material, and shape offered a particularly potent symbol of revolutionary panache as illustrated in one Red Guard's discussion:

> The badge I was wearing was one that I had dug down deep into my drawers to find. It was the nicest badge I had. The kind of badges we were wearing at the time were called, in the jargon of those in the know, "the eighty-round steamships." . . . These were the largest available. The size of these badges mattered in that the larger they were, the more loyal the wearer supposedly was—and certainly the more startlingly visible they were. . . . All in all, these badges were the newest, largest, and most fashionable of their kind at the time. There was not the slightest doubt that they were works of great craftsmanship. Stealing glances at

the "eighty-round" badge pinned to my clothes, how my classmates envied me! Especially pleased with myself, believing myself to be the most loyal to the cause, I would walk proudly with my head held high with more than a touch of exhibitionism. (Feng 1991:211)

Badges served as souvenirs that certified one's revolutionary credentials. At the same time, the *chuanlian* movement cast students into the role of tourist, an otherwise impossible luxury were it not framed as "revolutionary" tourism. Anthropological scholarship on tourism tells us that souvenirs encapsulate the experience of the journey, making the fantasy of the sacred available once reunited with the mundaneness of everyday life. Certainly, Red Guards appreciated more than the revolutionary sophistication the badges represented. At the time, revolutionary tourists were unable to risk the bourgeois nature of local mementos; such collection would have suggested a lack of revolutionary focus. By virtue of their ability to enhance one's revolutionary sophistication, badges were appropriate souvenirs. The production of souvenir badges was also profitable for various locales by advertising their regional commitment to the revolution.

One could further distinguish himself or herself by wearing badges in original ways. Respondents repeatedly talked about wearing their badges purposefully over the heart, in large numbers, and even pinned to the naked flesh. Zhou (1993) discusses a *People's Daily* article that recounts an episode in which a speaker inserted a badge the size of a bowl into the flesh on the left side of his chest. According to the article, the speaker started to bleed and was in great pain but continued to speak about loyalty and serving the people. Niu-Niu describes a similar scene she witnessed at a mass rally:

Carefully, he unfolded the paper to reveal a large pin with the image of Mao on it. Suddenly, he became nervous. Then, opening his shirt, he bared his chest. . . . His little fingers trembled feverishly as he held the sacred object. He turned his back again and, bowing deeply before Mao's poster, addressed it. "Mao, you are like a god to me, and I will do all in my power to please you. Accept the prayer of your humble servant." Saying this, he turned around and, before our disconcerted eyes, he pierced himself with the pin of the medallion, pinning it to his chest. . . . Seeing his convulsed face turn white made one feel sick, as if the pin had entered one's own flesh. . . . He wanted to smile, but he could only grimace from the pain. Later I learned from my grandfather that Chang Ta Pao had to go to Emergency because of the infection. The doctor who removed the pin was treated as a criminal: Chang Ta Pao would have preferred to die rather than to be separated from the medallion. . . . Because he was acclaimed by the populace as a model revolutionary, to let him die would have been to risk one's own life. (Niu-Niu 1995:21)

Tales of such ceremonial uses of Mao badges in life and death situations circulated throughout China during the Cultural Revolution, the moral of which was always Mao's supremacy, even when it meant the sacrifice of a life. Zhou (1993) recalls an incident in which Red Guards captured and tortured a member of another Red Guard faction. The captive attempted suicide by swallowing a Mao badge. Niu-Niu (1995) recounts "gawking" at the body of a counterrevolutionary who had punctured his torso with a Mao badge before he committed suicide. Revolutionary martyrs who died in a forest fire were claimed to have leaped into the flames shouting slogans and clutching their badges (Ma 1995).

As factional violence mounted, Red Guards used badges to identify political alliances. For example, former Red Guards remember Red Guard units that produced visually distinctive badges to mark themselves. Red Guards also distinguished factions by labeling badges with the names of their Red Guard units. Red Guard factions produced badges to demarcate political stances and typically distributed them only within a particular Red Guard unit. Respondents suggest that production of badge themes related to the incessant play of political proclamations slung between Red Guard units. Badges, likewise, represented counterclaims. In at least one case, a former Red Guard remembers competing factions stealing and defacing slogans on the backs of badges produced by competitors.

Virtues of Badges

The desire to authenticate redness drove Mao consumption to ever greater heights, resulting in a massive production of badges. Badge production spread to every work unit and political organization in China, and the trend to garner political legitimacy for badge text was common. This was most frequently accomplished by work units announcing their stamp of political approval through proclamations that Mao Zedong visited them. Such badges boasted, "Commemoration of Chairman Mao's inspection of . . ." When there were no recent inspections, workers commemorated anniversaries of such inspections. A handful of such badges includes the commentary "the happiest moment," suggesting a timelessness in local history. Interestingly, workers sought to distinguish political loyalty through local claims to fame in badges. One example is a badge featuring a petroleum drill worker urging his comrades to fight a fire. The text reads, "Commemoration of the third anniversary of the bloody battle against a sea of flames on June 22, Number 32111 Petroleum Drilling Team, February 12." Other examples include a badge that proposes to "hail the successful construction of the first large-scale hydraulic power station with self-designed and domestic equipment" and another "respectfully made by the Revolutionary Committee of Beijing Chemical Experiment Factory in commemoration of putting methanol into production." When there were no notable local events, virtually any activity was commemorated, as in the glow of a dark badge acknowledging the "Second Activists' Assembly of Studying and Applying Mao Zedong Thought of Shanghai Tool Factory."

Even those who did or could not participate in the national badge exchanges through chuanlian were eventually able to get diverse and distinctive badges from the outskirts. A Beijing respondent explains: "The new railway station at the time had trains coming and going to all corners of the country. Students who were participating in chuanlian would all come to Beijing and get off that railway station. Every day, I, like many other people, went to the railway station, bringing a lot of badges produced in Beijing. Most of them wanted Beijing badges, so I was able to exchange with students from all over the country."

As China's revolutionary liberator, Mao could be divorced, to some extent, from the trauma of the Cultural Revolution. As a political and filial figurehead, Mao held massive appeal. Barmé (1996) argues this point particularly well, suggesting that Mao was effectively marketed and received as leader, teacher, philosopher, nationalist—in Barmé's terms, an "everyMao." Rae Yang illustrates such intimacy when she describes her dual love for Mao:

He was, on the one hand, the radiant sun in the sky, giving life to everything on earth. This Mao I loved as

millions of Chinese did at the time. . . . But behind
this Mao there was another: a secret, sweetheart hero
of a fifteen-year-old girl. . . . This Mao, to me, was not
the radiant sun but a vulnerable man, a tragic hero.
. . . I loved Mao by day and played the role of the hero
at night. The two heroes of mine did not seem to get
along. I began to have insomnia. (R. Yang 1997:112)

Landsberger also acknowledges the graphic concordance
between Mao and the people:

And yet, despite the apparent distance between the
Leader and the Led, there was something in the images featuring Mao that struck a chord with the people.
. . . The "imaged" Mao somehow remained united with
the people, whether he inspected fields, shook hands
with the peasants, sat down with them, and shared a
cigarette with them; whether he was dressed in military uniform, discussing strategy with military leaders, inspected the rank-and-file, or mingled with
contingents of Red Guards; whether he headed a col-
umn of representatives of the national minorities, or
received a delegation of foreign visitors. (Landsberger
1996:208)

This prismatic Mao was ultimately adaptable and readily
consumed in the critical scramble to secure political legitimacy. Mao consumption may also have been particularly
helpful to students who were less inclined toward destruction, as indicated by their loyalty. Chan, Rosen, and Unger
(1980:429) point out the discomfort exhibited by middle-
class youth participating in the "red terror": "Objects they
were confiscating were rather similar to the items in their
own homes."

Vicious Cycles

The competition to prove true redness was an endless cycle that relied on such "esoteric criteria" (Appadurai 1992) that made authentication impossible. Despite efforts to the contrary, Red Guard units were indistinguishable. Anita Chan (1992) notes this irony, commenting on the difficulty of discerning factions by virtue of the identical nature of their efforts to protect Mao. Participants constantly invented "sumptuary laws" (McCracken 1988) to distinguish their revolutionary fervor only to find their efforts co-opted by competing degrees of redness.

The mass production and circulation of Mao badges led to greater accessibility to badges among the larger population, democratizing political virtue through what Douglas and Isherwood (1989) term a "distributive justice." Of course, the mass consumption of Mao propaganda served official ambitions, and it did not guarantee status protection. However, Mao consumption allowed (albeit limited) opportunities to move beyond passive resignation to redefine oneself by virtue of effort and novelty rather than the static blood lineage theory. Particularly when backed by political winds favoring one's participation over background, this opportunity could make an enormous difference in the course of one's Cultural Revolution career.

5

Aluminum

Gods

Mao Badges
and Chinese
Ritual Life

In a discussion of local propaganda in Chinese culture, Lynn White (1979) points out that any centralized communication tactic is compromised by competing loyalties in an individual's background, obligations, and opportunities. Chinese citizens did not passively receive badges as emblems of devotion; instead, they creatively consumed and exchanged badges, using them as a currency to manipulate the system and circumvent official rhetoric.

Badges came to be valued political safeguards as citizens rebounded from the terrorist activities of the Red Guards. Though badges were not impervious to political criticism, they did offer a stabilizing force amid the radically shifting political currents. Unlike the transient nature of big-character posters, badges could not accommodate the dizzying pace of the shifting winds of Cultural Revolution movements. They were, quite literally, metal, not paper, tigers and were not easily changed or destroyed. While big-character posters were often shrouded in anonymity, badges could never be anonymous. Though the manufacturer might remain unnamed, badge functions went well beyond manufacture as they were worn, traded, and displayed. As a result, badge text, both written and visual, was essentially innocuous. Badge text did not typically invite the rampant criticism that was so much a part of the revolutionary struggle. The very fact that badges were less of a political liability in that they did not ensnare the "feast of criticism" (Leijonhufvud 1990), so prevalent during the Cultural Revolution, allowed the extension of their functions as consumer objects as well as collectibles. Badges, like posters, were a socializing catalyst; devoid of critical content, badges served as a route to more entrepreneurial forms of consumption.

The constant production of Mao badges ruptured Mao's image from the exclusive context of political virtue and generated a perceptual shift of the meaning of that image. By providing a constant, immediate testimonial to Mao Zedong, badges evolved into a disguise as much as a proclamation, concealing activities that preserved the pre–Cultural Revolution norms of everyday social and ritual life.

The ambitious and, often, covert collection and exchange of Mao badges reflects pre–Cultural Revolution conceptualizations of reciprocal social relations. The material exchanges of Mao badges suggest a layer of sociability and trust as well as an innovative method of getting things done outside of official channels. By enveloping Mao badges into indigenous, potentially subversive legacies of social exchange, Chinese citizens fractured a strident nationalist ideology. The obligation to preface everyday life with Mao was transformed into the luxury of safeguarding everyday life with Mao.

Political Ritual

The perpetual objectification of political virtue became an orthopraxy that can be described as "political ritual." Aijmer (1996:218) offers a compelling description of this process in his deconstruction of imagery during the Cultural Revolution: "Whenever the pragmatic construction of political celebration merges with intuitively created images in the cultural symbolic order to form consciously informed and yet culturally endowed icons, we encounter a phenomenon we may call political ritual."

The ambitious political ritualization that followed the establishment of revolutionary committees resulted in a sometimes unforgiving formalization of Mao's image and words. Ma (1995), punished for equating Jiang Qing with the Empress Dowager, shared his imprisonment with a man who accidentally shouted, "Down with Chairman Mao" when he meant to say "Down with Liu Shaoqi" during a heated argument. Another prisoner had slandered Mao by saying that Mao had once served as propaganda minister for the Nationalists. Niu-Niu (1995:22) recollects watching a peasant being beaten for proudly declaring that he named his son Mao Zedong. Her grandmother explained the error: "He's an illiterate peasant. . . . How could he dare to give that name to his no-account son?"

Children, too young to understand the dangers of objectifying Mao, were often a liability:

> There were a few children only five or six years old who were labeled anti-Revolutionaries at the beginning of the Revolution. Through simple curiosity, or by parroting what they heard at home, or testing their own creative power, some of these children shouted anti-Revolutionary slogans: "Down with Chairman Mao!" or "Chairman Mao is a rotten egg!" bringing punishment on their entire family. (Luo 1990:273)

Zhou (1993) relays a story in which an entire family faced persecution for a similar incident during a family gathering in which a playful child, seeing a big Chairman Mao badge on the wall, jumped on the table, waving her hand and shouting "Mao." Afraid the little girl would step on a piece of glass on the table, her father told her that if she didn't come down, the "tiger" would bite her. This incident was used later as evidence of the family's counter-revolutionary tendencies.

Luo remembers a neighborhood physician imprisoned for wrapping his galoshes in a newspaper containing Mao's photo. She later recounts the consequences of her own joke to a fellow worker:

> Chairman Mao finished his nationwide inspection and published his "Newest Instructions" when he arrived back in Beijing: "I would describe the political situation as 'major good,' not 'minor good.' But in a few months, it will be even better." . . . I mimicked Chairman Mao's quotation in a teasing way to one of my colleagues: "I would describe the meteorological situation as 'major cold' not 'minor cold.' But in a few months, it will be even colder." . . . He laughed when he heard me say this, but then reported it to the secretary. I was considered an anti-revolutionary who attacked Chairman Mao. (Luo 1990:185)

Rae Yang remembers a "gigantic counter-revolutionary incident" among the peasants with whom she worked:

> Overnight, almost every house in the region was searched and who knows how many poor peasants were implicated. . . . Their crime was sticking needles into Chairman Mao's face and body. In fact, they did this

unintentionally, for in those days Chairman Mao's pictures were all over the newspapers the villagers had always used for wallpaper. So after the women sewed, if they stuck the needles in the wall at the wrong places, poor peasants became active counter-revolutionaries and were shut up in the cowshed for months. (R. Yang 1997:242)

Citizens guarded everyday interaction with an ample degree of paranoia. One young girl recalls the fear of being associated with the subversive use of Mao after coloring the sun black because she had no colored crayons:

When I showed it to Professor Yang, she turned pale and asked, "Why is it black?" I looked down at my shoes and told her why. Professor Yang made sure that no one was watching and promptly tore up my drawing, cramming the pieces into her pocket. Without a word, she led me into the street, as if she were afraid of something. We came to a little store where she pointed to a packet of crayons, made sure that there was a red one in there, then offered it to me. "Here, Niu-Niu, never color the sun black again." (Niu-Niu 1995:62)

Another Red Guard remembers a roommate imprisoned for defacing a Mao portrait. He had finished writing a big-character poster and when shaking it to dry, he splashed ink on the portrait. He quickly hid the portrait in his blanket and forgot about it. People's Liberation Army (PLA) soldiers discovered the picture and sentenced the man to ten years of prison (Feng 1991).

The adequacy of one's management of Mao was a frightful and constant topic under the banner of the new wave of political rituals. The intense ritualization proved challenging for many Cultural Revolution participants haunted by untamed, counter-revolutionary thoughts, or what was known as *shan nian*, flash of thought (M. Yang 1994). One Red Guard explains:

> You see, during the Cultural Revolution there were a lot of photographs. The thought "Chairman Mao looks like a pig" occasionally flashed across my mind. I had to push away that thought. It was the same with Lin Biao. It flashed across my mind that he looked like a dog with a wagging tail. Oh, I was scared of myself. You see, we often went on propaganda tours and slept together, and I often talked in my sleep. I was afraid that such a thought would leak out and other people would overhear it. I knew a lot of people were caught for counter-revolutionary activities based on evidence like this. I feared being thrown in prison, so every morning when I woke up I asked the people around whether I had said anything in my dreams during the night. (Chan 1985:181)

In a poignant internal dialogue reflecting the fragility of political ritual, another Red Guard struggles with her insurgent thoughts:

> Every member of the Propaganda Team was required to keep Chairman Mao's thoughts in mind every minute of the day. Such work kept me physically and spiritually exhausted all the time. . . . I do not remember why, but I was asked to hold Mao's portrait while carrying a rifle on my shoulder. That was my first time holding the portrait. It was a frightening experience. I felt like I was being assigned as a bodyguard for Mao. After the team leader told me about my new position and I left his office, Chinese characters started coming

unbidden into my head. I could see them, one by one: *qiang* (gun), *bi* (kill). *Qiang bi*. And then a sentence: *Qiang bi Mao zhu xi* (assassinate Chairman Mao). I was terrified by these thoughts. . . . I tried to hide my thoughts by forcing myself to think of the line "Mao Zedong's thought is great." But the harder I tried to think the "proper" thoughts, the more the other words returned. . . . I told myself that no one would ever know if I didn't speak my thoughts out loud. But how could I hold them inside? They were too powerful. I decided that the only way out was suicide. (Wen 1995:91)

Aluminum Gods

Paralleling Mao's image with traditional icons, Landsberger (1996) suggests that Mao acted as surrogate for the traditional Chinese kitchen god, a deity that demanded loyalty and devotion to ensure supreme guardianship over domestic affairs. Landsberger further argues that the ritualized deification of Mao distanced him from the mundaneness of everyday life. Mao's image was ever present, but the man himself was, in Landsberger's terms, "in absentia." As Mao's image obscured traditional ritual icons, individuals summoned Mao for what Weiner (1992) terms "cosmological authentication." Individuals invested Mao with a shielding quality that connoted strength and protection in forging ahead in the turmoil of the Cultural Revolution. Niu-Niu (1995), for example, describes looking at Mao's portrait for encouragement in managing the turmoil of her family's victimization. Ma (1995:19) applies a Mao quotation to stimulate his work in the countryside: "Bathed in sweat, I spurred myself on with a quote from Chairman Mao: 'When the enemy is at his strongest and you are in trouble, that is when his problems begin and the situation turns in your favor. A favorable situation and a return of initiative comes from perseverance and hard work.'"

The ceaseless ritualization of Mao had a cumulative effect by which the consumption of Mao's image represented a formality that, in itself, became somewhat mundane. Turner's (1974) classic anthropological analysis of ritual offers an instructive view of political ritual during the Cultural Revolution. Turner argues that ritual activity invokes an ambiguity that suspended the superstructure (normative behaviors, status hierarchies, and relationships). However, unlike Turner's small-scale societies where ritual activity was only occasional, the political rituals of the Cultural Revolution were constant. Everyday life was politicized to the nth degree during the Cultural Revolution. It seems fair to apply Turner's notion of limenality to Cultural Revolution participants whose survival depended on political ritual. During the Cultural Revolution, the ritual never ended; the incessant nature of political ritual stunted transition to a fixed and meaningful role. Despite official ambitions to the contrary, orthodoxy did not submerge orthopraxy. The saturation of the social by the political did not necessarily result in conquest by the latter. In the same way that Mao's image permeated private life, citizens domesticated that image to circumvent the impossible feat of subsuming the orthodoxy of the Cultural Revolution.

Mao's image came to be necessary to get by in everyday life; the synergistic nature of endless political ritual transferred Mao's sacrosanct image to the realm of the profanely ordinary. As in the case with one Red Guard, political rituals privileged appearances:

A week after the opening of school, the professor announced that after we had chanted, "Good morning, Mao," we should all answer four questions every morning: "Do you love Mao? Will you follow Mao all your life? Are you a good child of Mao's? Do you have something to confess to Mao?" For the first three questions, you had to answer without hesitation. "Yes, I love the great Mao, I'll follow him all my life. I'll do everything I can to be a good child of Mao." As for the fourth, that was stickier. When the children had been fighting or had not done their homework, they had to say, "I have some faults to confess to Mao; yesterday I had a fight with a friend. . . . I talked during class. . . . I ask Mao to pardon me, and I ask all my classmates to forgive me, too. I will improve immediately." This was the ritual that took place every morning before the lessons began. Even if we didn't understand everything, we had to repeat the answers by heart, for Mao had said, "If you understand, do better; if you don't understand, obey and understand later." (Niu-Niu 1995:96)

The domestic mundaneness of Mao's image heightened following students' exodus to the countryside, where peasants were enjoying a modicum of freedom. Ma remembers surprise at the cavalier management of political dictum during a typical study meeting in the countryside:

This first lesson in class struggle took us by surprise, for the minute the meeting was called to order, the poor and lower-middle-class herdsmen began to giggle, goof off, brag, hold spitting contests, or stretch out to catch up on their sleep, clutching the grimiest "Little Red Books" I'd ever seen. Once again the newspapers had fed us a crock. (Ma 1995:12)

Ma later describes a typical Mongolian home :

As I surveyed the seedy yurt, I took mental inventory of possessions: a couple of wooden chests whose paint was peeling; a piece of red cloth on which thirty or

more Mao badges had been pinned: an assortment of
cooking utensils in a smoky cupboard; some patched,
dirty flour sacks; and a rug covered with goat hairs,
scraps of paper, cigarette butts, cinders, and slivers of
goatchips—all, of course, pervaded by the stench of his
children's urine. (Ma 1995:22)

Indeed, it was this very mundaneness of political ritual
on which the Maoists depended to subdue the rampant chaos
of the early years of the Cultural Revolution. The rote necessity of Mao's image offered a thin veneer, a necessary
public display that obliged an element of autonomy in the
maintenance of social worlds.

Mao badges offered Chinese citizens a refreshing and
friendly diversion from the anxieties of displaying correct
behavior. Acting out the revolution with a tangible sign
bypassed the messiness of language and externalized political virtue. As talismans of political loyalty that presented
an immediate statement of political ideology, badges evolved
into accouterments of the highest order. Narratives regarding the absence of a badge infer a sense of political nudity.
Yungsheng Chen, an artist whose paintings of his Red Guard
experiences are done from Taiwan, where he fled during the
Cultural Revolution, exemplifies this in his painting entitled *Red Badges*, the caption of which reads: "In order to
exhibit one's unlimited, steadfast, and absolute loyalty to
Mao Zedong, the entire population was obliged to wear a
loyalty badge when going outside. Otherwise, one might be
exposed as one who 'had problems' in his ideology" (Y. Chen
1971:52).

In a criticism of her treatment by fellow Red Guards, a
Red Guard from a competing faction reveals the panic of
going outside without her Mao badge. During an invasion
by another revolutionary faction, in the midst of being hit,

kicked, and dragged away while Red Guards destroyed her home, she dropped her Mao badge. She writes:

> Seizing the front of my clothes, the tall one said, "Get moving!" Finding my badge with a quotation from Chairman Mao on the ground, I stooped to pick it up. Someone then hit me, shouting at me angrily, "Get moving, quick!" "Don't you people see you have dropped my quotation badge which I should be wearing?" I said. (*Samples of Red Guard Publications II*, 1967:19)

In a short story devoted solely to Mao badges, the narrator's wife chastises his obsession with badges after she learns that he took all of the family's badges to the market to exchange them for one impressive badge:

> "You've got Mao buttons on the brain!" she said. "You never do what you're supposed to when you get home from work—and tonight, of all things, you run out into the streets to swap buttons. Don't you know what kind of riffraff you could have run into out there? And you took the kid's and my buttons too! If they'd been stolen, what would we have worn tomorrow? People would say I'd gone without my button because I didn't love Chairman Mao. They'd arrest me as a counter-revolutionary, and there wouldn't be anybody here to cook for you when you got home from work every day." (Feng 1985:23)

As objects that were worn, badges allowed an escape from exposure, even if limited. Of course, the intense formalization of the Mao interpretive minefield of the red vanguard resulted in very little politically safe space. Like any medium of Mao's image, badges required copious management. Sun-Childers illustrates the danger of dropping a badge:

> Early one spring evening I sat in the barracks on Mama's bed, awaiting her return from the rice paddy. Women came in, dirty and muddy from preparing the paddy for planting. Mama came up to me wearing a beautiful new Chairman Mao pin on her jacket. Rays of light shone in a halo around Chairman Mao's golden silhouette. A red sun rose above him, and below him was a sapphire blue ocean. Such a special pin! Chairman Mao's pins were everyone's treasures; we all collected, traded, and wore them proudly. I made such a big fuss over Mama's pin that she took it off her jacket and bent forward to pin it on me. "You can have it, little Jaia," she said. Then something terrible happened. Mama dropped the pin on the muddy dirt floor, face-down! Mama dropped Chairman Mao's face in the mud! I knew you must never do this. Mama knew too. She glanced nervously around like a criminal and quickly picked up the pin. She sneakily wiped Chairman Mao's mud-stained face on her sleeve. Then she pinned it on my jacket. But I was very angry. Teacher Yi had taught us you can drop anything except Chairman Mao's pin and his little red book. This was anti-revolutionary! It meant you opposed Chairman Mao in your heart! I looked up at Mama. Word by word, with her comrades nearby, I accused her: "You do not love Chairman Mao!" Her body froze guiltily; people looked over. Mama couldn't even look me, her five-year-old daughter, in the eye. Luckily, none of her comrades saw her crime. Years later I realized Mama narrowly escaped what might have been a political disaster. (Sun-Childers 1995:39)

In his short story, Feng also illustrates the severity of

dropping a Mao badge through his protagonist, Kong, who finally finds a badge that would inspire envy among his workmates:

"Hey, everybody," someone shouted, "come see Mr. Kong's Mao button!" In no time flat he was surrounded by a crowd. People were jostling each other and craning their necks to see. They were looking at his button with amazement and envy, and at him with a new respect. Everyone was yelling, which attracted more people. "Now that's a big button. Where did you get it?" "Mr. Kong, you're a real go-getter!" "Of course! I am loyal to Chairman Mao," he said with a smug laugh, keeping one hand on the button in case anyone tried to snatch it. Some people tried to move his fingers out of the way so that they could get a better look at the button; others tried to peek at the back to find out where it was made . . . the excitement he was causing was a sign that his button was without compare not only at the office, but probably in the whole city. Unless someone made a button as big as a crock lid, which only a giant could wear. . . . Unable to stand it any longer, he began to wriggle his way out of the unbearable crush, away from the hands that were pulling on him. . . . Finally he squeezed his way out like a noodle out of a noodle machine. He was exhilarated. But just then he heard a clank, as though a heavy metal platter had fallen to the ground. Then he heard it rolling around. He did not realize what the sound was until he reached up and found that his Mao button was gone. "On, no! My button fell off!" he cried. Everyone froze and he began a frantic search. It was not on the ground in front of him, so he stepped back to turn around and look behind him. He felt something hard and slippery underfoot. "Oh no! You're standing on a button with a portrait of Chairman Mao!" he heard a woman say, before he could grasp what had happened. In terror he looked down and saw the Mao button under his heel. He should have been able to lift his foot quickly, but it was as unresponsive as a piece of wood. His body went limp and his weight sank into the offending leg. With all eyes riveted upon him, he stood rooted to the spot. This blunder was a heinous crime that brought him to the brink of destruction. There is no need to recount the details here. Suffice it to say that he recovered from his Mao-button mania and came to look upon these former objects of affection with fear and trembling. (Feng 1985:27)

Respondents also remember porcelain badges, in particular, as politically risky. Porcelain badges were burned or baked, an unsuitable processing of Mao's image. In addition, porcelain badges were likely to break if dropped, thereby entailing a much greater liability.

Compared to many forms of propaganda, however, badges were a relatively safe medium. They were typically small enough to negotiate missteps in handling them. They also were clasped to one's body with a pin attached to the back. One Red Guard illustrates the durability of badges compared to other forms of propaganda in a story about field training with the PLA. Initially disappointed that a soldier's Mao bust outshone his Mao badge, ultimately the badge proved the safer strategy:

Our platoon was led by a red flag carrier who was immediately followed by a tall soldier carrying a huge bust of Chairman Mao. . . . While marching, we would shout slogans in unison, recite quotations of the Chairman's, and sing revolutionary songs. . . . Now, of course, in hindsight, it all seems ridiculous. What enemy were we talking about? . . . Nonetheless, from early morning until it grew dark outside, we didn't feel the least bit tired. But the platoon leader, fearing that the tall soldier carrying the porcelain bust of Chairman Mao was exhausted, began to look for someone to replace him. Immediately all the soldiers in the platoon jumped up and began to clamor, each vying for the privilege of carrying the bust. We students, too, all threw our hats into the ring, hoping to take on that honored responsibility, since everyone believed that whoever in the end successfully competed for the honor would be the most loyal to Chairman Mao among us. But to everyone's disbelief, the tall soldier who had been carrying the porcelain bust refused to relinquish his responsibility, declaring in an agitated, booming voice, "I am going to protect Chairman Mao on the new Long March." . . . His pledge filled me with admiration for him. His loyalty and sincerity made the "eighty-yuan" badge on my chest seem very ordinary and unworthy of attention.

After endless hours of walking, the soldier grows weary and drops the porcelain bust:

Breaking the icon of the Chairman was a dreadful crime of hideous proportions. Without waiting for us to wake up to what had happened, the tall fellow suddenly fell to the ground and, kneeling in front of the broken pieces of the bust, began to beg forgiveness! And the platoon leader, who had let such an appalling thing happen, involuntarily fell to the ground himself, begging pardon too! Then the whole platoon, without waiting for the order, fell to its knees. A short while afterward, the second platoon arrived on the scene. Seeing us all kneeling on the ground, they wondered what had happened. . . . The second platoon leader walked over and, seeing the shattered remains of the bust, fell to his knees at once without a single word. This, in turn, set his own men to falling down on their knees in one great swoosh . . . the third platoon and its leader (also) fell to their knees like a row of frightened dominoes— everyone wanted to be the first to drop down, for that would mean that he was the most thoroughly loyal, the most resolute. (Feng 1991:213)

As medal plates worn on the chest, badges connoted a uniquely impenetrable shield. Ma (1995), for example, recalls preparing for the countryside by packing money, ration books, clothes, backpacks, compasses, knives, medicine, and Chairman Mao badges. Gao describes his preparedness for the adventure of *chuanlian*, the "revolutionary exchange": "bedrolls strapped to our backs, armbands on ours sleeves, and Chairman Mao buttons on our chests" (1987:127). Liang remembers: "I pinned my collection of Chairman Mao buttons in display fashion onto a large handkerchief, folding it carefully and putting it into the pocket of the beat-up cotton-padded overcoat I had borrowed from Father. I wanted to be ready for anything" (Liang and Shapiro 1983:112).

By virtue of their physicality, badges embodied an instrumentality that far surpassed other forms of propaganda. Badges were particularly effective ritual signifiers. As small, self-contained objects, they offered the advantage of condensing the increasingly elusive political ideology of the Cultural Revolution. As emblems that were displayed, badges were immediate visual codes of loyalty. The fact that individuals displayed them on their bodies posed an additional semiotic advantage by suggesting that badges were an extension of one's being. By virtue of their celebrated legacy as signals of political validity, badges were a powerfully authoritative medium of identification. This authority imbued badges with a refractive power that held the potential to both divert and shield.

Maoified Rituals

By 1969, Chinese citizens elaborated on the custodial dimension of Mao's image and thought to realize ambitions and expressions that were politically suspect during the Cultural Revolution. Students commonly adopted Mao's works as a conduit to perform varied educational exercises, and at least one teacher used the practice of "red diaries" during the Cultural Revolution as a technique to improve students' composition skills (M. Yang 1994).

More compelling testimony to the use of Mao as a shield is in the continued self-study of English via Mao's writings. The study of English was forbidden during the Cultural Revolution, though students confess to studying English through the English version of Mao's Little Red Book (Wen 1995) and, curiously, English does appear on certain badges. A self-taught student during the Cultural Revolution asked a professor to teach her Western languages. He initially refused, explaining, "If I do this, I could be accused of using Western bourgeois culture to pollute the minds of young people. A foreign language, by nature, is anti-Revolutionary. It's like poison." The student countered, "Chairman Mao's quotations have been translated into dozens of languages. You can always say that you're teaching foreign languages in service of the revolution" (Luo 1990:217). Another Red Guard remembers a similar discussion with his father, who had urged him to study English:

"Studying English is not allowed. No English materials are available in any stores. What do you want me
to do?" Dad interrupted me, "The *Complete Works of
Mao* is available in English." I felt outraged. "I don't
have spare money for such stupid books." "Nothing is
stupid as long as it can help you learn something. The
English version of Mao's collections is idiomatic." Dad
crawled under the bed and pulled out a wooden trunk.
He took a book out and handed it to me. "Here is my
English version of Mao's works. I bought it before I left
Beijing. It's yours now. Studying English is forbidden.
Studying Mao's teachings is not. There is a Chinese
set of Mao's works at home. You can study English by
reading both versions." What else could I say? When I
returned to work, I read the Chinese version when the
leaders of the factory were present. Otherwise I read
the English version. Gradually the leaders began to
think of me as a good youth, trying to reform myself
and willing to break off my relationship with my father. I impressed them with my study of Mao's teachings. (Wen 1995:154)

On the most basic level, badges held an esthetic appeal
that was inappropriate in any other context during the Cultural Revolution. At the same time that the fashionable
cultivation of one's physical appearance was prohibited, Mao
badges became increasingly elaborate. Badges display a vo-
luminous array of colors, materials, and designs that were
not allowed in everyday attire. At least one respondent discusses the most esthetically extravagant badges as problem-
atic, suggesting that they were kept in secret because they
might attract too much attention on the dull-colored background of Mao suits and army uniforms.

A more provocative use of Mao to shield traditional

customs lies in the use of Mao's image to hide traditional religious icons. In at least one case, the use of Mao as a subversive shield was quite literal:

> In those days almost every family in the country had some kind of shrine or picture of Mao in the house. In our house we had a statue of Mao, sitting on a small covered stand under a glass case. Under the stand for Mao was my mother's statue of the Buddha. Every morning and night when she bowed to Mao, she was actually praying to the Buddha behind him. In front of the statue was a bronze incense burner that had belonged to my mother's ancestors. (Wen 1995:141)

Sun-Childers (1995) relays a similar anecdote, describing a Buddhist statue she found behind Mao's picture on his grandmother's altar.

Chinese rituals, particularly weddings and spring festival celebrations, were vulnerable to accusations of excessive bourgeois and feudal display. Take, for example, a plan among Red Guards to "revolutionize the spring festival":

> The revolutionary situation is excellent and getting better. How should we approach the upcoming 1967 spring festival in the midst of this Great Proletarian Cultural Revolutionary high tide? We—the revolutionary rebels—reply without any hesitations: by making it a target of revolution! The spring festival is one of the spiritual shackles forced upon the working people for millennia by the exploiting classes. In the old society, the spring festival was heaven for the rich and hell for the poor. Our ancestors sacrificed blood and sweat, yet for generations got no more than the "freedom" to labor like oxen, like horses. During the seventeen years that have passed since liberation, a small handful of

party-persons in power taking the capitalist road have utilized the forces of old social conventions represented by the spring festival to praise the bourgeois lifestyle of eating, drinking, amusing oneself, and having fun, and to faithfully work in the service of the exploiting classes. They utilize the spring festival to engage in feudal superstitious activities on a massive scale, to beseech the gods and sacrifice to ancestors, to promote hypocritical etiquette, to invite guests and present gifts, to get drunk, gamble and eat and drink excessively, and in the this way to turn the spring festival into a marketplace for the unchecked spread of the four olds . . . Can we still put up with a spring festival that is so heavily tainted with the hues of feudalism, capitalism, and revisionism? No we cannot! Absolutely not! We must act in accordance with Chairman Mao's teaching and promote the revolutionization of people's thinking in the course of the Great Cultural Revolution. We must make the spring festival a target of revolution! (Schoenhals 1996:223)

In the same year, the government issued a circular to cancel spring festival holidays. Mao icons served the dual function of obscuring ritual excess and supplanting it. For example, Zhai (1992) recalls an elaborate countryside wedding diluted by presents of Mao badges. Respondents married during the Cultural Revolution repeatedly note the abundance of presents, all variations of Mao badges, busts, and writings. Afraid to dispose of the venerated objects, newlyweds regularly recycled Mao wedding gifts when friends or family members married. Luo (1990:14) describes a typical Cultural Revolution wedding photograph, abundant with the pomp and fanfare expected of wedding ceremonies; however, the regalia had been appropriately Maoified: "The bride and groom posed with red bags at their waists, Chairman Mao's picture pinned to their chests, Little Red Books held in one hand over their shoulders, and stacks of Chairman Mao's works in the other. A sunflower in the background represented their loyalty to the Red Sun."

Acknowledging the necessity of including Mao badges and Little Red Books in family and wedding photographs, one photographer remembers collecting and displaying his own Mao badges as props to solicit customers. He states, "Life size Mao Zedong badges among photographers served the same purpose as wedding dresses and backgrounds" (Zhou 1993). Zhou also tells a story of a young couple who married in 1968 and received "red gifts," including twenty-four sets of selected readings, thirty-two copies of Mao's quotation book, and one hundred and sixty-seven Mao badges. Flattered but dismayed by the excess, the bride asked the groom, "Such a pile of books and badges! They are not edible, and we cannot sell or throw them away. Where can we put them?" The groom admonished her, "You cannot say such things when you go outside." Finally, they decided to give the pile of revolutionary gifts to another pair of newlyweds weeks later.

Gao remembers his reprieve from Red Guard activities to return to his hometown for the Chinese spring festival where the revolutionary staging of the town defied the private celebratory atmosphere:

Chairman Mao quotations in fresh red paint and pictures of Chairman Mao captioned with the character for loyalty on a red heart adorned the walls of the villages along the road. . . . Almost everyone in the streets was wearing a Chairman Mao portrait on a necklace, and some of the older people held the portrait up in front of their chests as they walked. . . . Mama had bought us a quarter of a pig this year. When she came

on spring festival morning to eat *jiaozi*, she also
brought gifts from the tank regiment that supported
Papa: a bag of exquisite Chairman Mao quotation
books, half the size of regular ones, and some large
Chairman Mao badges, one as big as a soup bowl. The
metal used to make the badges reputedly came from
B-52s shot down in Vietnam. My sisters, brothers, and
I were so happy that we capered around to the dance
called "On the golden hill of Beijing." (Gao 1987:32)

The circulation of Mao badges as gifts during the Cultural Revolution suggests the saliency of traditional understandings of reciprocity that bound family and community
members in a system of respect and reliance. Such exchanges
encouraged a deeper reading of the establishment and maintenance of personal relationships during the Cultural Revolution. Certainly, during this time, any relationships were
fraught with danger. Encouraged to monitor and report on
one another, even relatives represented political liabilities.
Ma (1995:185), for example, reveals the public negotiation
of family dynamics in a letter written to him in prison from
his mother: "You claim that in subjective terms you're neither anti-party nor anti–Chairman Mao. Then how do you
explain your actions, since most are in opposition to Chairman Mao and Mao Zedong Thought? We tried to get you to
spend more time studying the works of Chairman Mao instead of those rotten novels, which clouded your mind with
feudal, fascist, corrupt thoughts."

Another Red Guard illustrates the fairly common act of
disowning one's family in the following dialogue with his
father during the Cultural Revolution: "Listen carefully! . . .
Chairman Mao has already urged me to rebel. How dare
you try to restrain and discipline me? . . . I am not your son
anymore. I belong to Chairman Mao and to the Revolution"
(Wen 1995:60).

The intense stress involved in personal relationships makes the hint of reciprocity all the more remarkable. At the very least, badge exchanges suggested a discernment between public political rituals and the machinations of everyday life. The movement of Mao badges among families opened a sphere of relationships that were otherwise suspect during the Cultural Revolution.

Black Market Badges

Individuals also used badges to get goods and services that were otherwise difficult to obtain, particularly during the demise of chuanlian, when Red Guards were no longer given free meals or travel. Gao describes giving a badge to a helpful policeman who bought him noodles after Gao had exhausted his resources during chuanlian:

> Leaving my three companions sitting on the waiting room floor, I bravely set out alone for the Municipal Party Committee headquarters to beg for some help. An official there put me to bed in a room with other Red Guards. The next morning, he gave me breakfast, eight yuan, and eight jin worth of grain coupons. Elated, I took a bus back to the railway station. My comrades were not in the waiting room. I spotted them on the sidewalk talking to a policeman. Delta was showing the policeman a Jinggang Mountain badge and saying, "We haven't eaten for a day. Please trade us a little money and a few grain coupons for this badge. Normally it's worth ten or twelve small badges." The policeman led them into a restaurant and ordered three bowls of noodles. I appeared at the table. Proudly, I offered to repay the policeman for the food. He refused. I unpinned my prized golden Chairman Mao badge from my chest and insisted he take it. (Gao 1987:172)

Liang details a transaction with a railway guard in which he offered a Mao badge to ride illegally on the train:

> I reached deep into my pocket and took out my handkerchief, exposing my treasures to his greedy gaze. His hands were big and greasy, and I sat in horror as he fondled my prizes, my heart jumping as he paused before each jewel, afraid that that would be the one I would have to sacrifice. While I could not bear to part with a single one, I could also hear the loudspeaker calling, "All Red Guards without Peking identification cards, please get off immediately," and I was afraid he might pay attention and make a connection between the announcements and my presence. So I babbled incoherently, trying to distract him . . . and he wavered interminably, hating to lose any of them just as much as I did. Finally he unclasped one of the Jinggang Mountain buttons. . . . I thought I would die, for I only had three from Jinggang Mountain. At the same time I felt I would have given him the whole handkerchief-full if only he would not throw me off the train. So I watched in private agony as he pinned the button onto his blue worker's overcoat, smiling and chatting as if I were his guest for Sunday tea. (Liang and Shapiro 1983:114)

Similarly, Ling (1972:286) describes his use of badges as bargaining chips in exchange for a ride: "I pinned all the badges I had 'earned' giving bicycle rides on a red armband and, when I saw a truck, waved the armband so that all the badges rattled. If the truck stopped, I would climb aboard and haggle with the driver about the 'price.'"

As Mao deflated Red Guard claims to redness, individuals continued to use badges to gain goods and services that were otherwise difficult to obtain. No doubt that many clever entrepreneurs capitalized upon the demand for Mao badges as Ling (1972) did himself, offering "sick or limp stragglers" a ride on his bicycle, accepting Mao badges as his only reward. Li (1993:11) reports on a Beijing homemaker whose shabby living conditions prompted her to offer housing authorities a gift of Mao badges; five days later, officials upgraded the woman to a spacious apartment.

Zhou (1993) relates a story of a factory manager who controlled distribution of Mao badges and used his position to give family members badges through the "back door." On one occasion, the manager's sister-in-law approached him to obtain one of the factory's newest badges. The manager was unsure; he had only a limited number of badges for the workers. The manager finally decided to give the badge of one of the workers, Wu, to his sister-in-law. Wu later attended a workers' conference and realized he was not given a badge. Obsessed with worry that he had done something wrong, he had difficulty eating and sleeping and lost weight from the stress. Other workers noticed that Wu huddled in the corner at political meetings, and became introverted and less active during work hours. Other workers began to gossip, and Wu's actions were monitored closely. Finally, Wu approached the factory's Revolutionary Committee with a self-criticism. He confessed every memory of wrongdoing: fighting with neighbors, keeping several yuan he had found. The committee determined that since Wu was so obviously burdened by guilt, he was not disclosing everything. He was subsequently persecuted.

Chang discusses what she interprets as the commodification of Mao, describing her brother's dealings in Mao badges to obtain money to continue his scientific experiments. She refers to the "clandestine" nature of badge exchange, explaining that collecting during the Cultural Revolution had been banned as bourgeois. In her final analysis, she gives a more explicit link between the Mao trade and capitalism:

> To get money for his experiments, he even dealt in Mao badges. Many factories had stopped normal production to produce aluminum badges with Mao's head on them. Collecting of any kind, including stamps and paintings, had been banned as "bourgeois habit." So people's instinct for collecting turned to this sanctioned object—although they could only deal in it clandestinely. Jin-ming made a small fortune. Little did the Great Helmsman know that even the image of his head had become a piece of property for capitalist speculation, the very activity he had tried so hard to stamp out. (Chang 1991:369)

As Chang points out, the excessive production of badges resulted in a wastefulness that contradicted dogma on revolutionary economism. The collection and display of badges smacked of a bourgeois conspicuous consumption that the government only tolerated in the pursuit of a cult of loyalty toward Mao. One collector remembers his pseudo-political intrigue with badges:

> Many Red Guards stayed at the meeting hall of my parents' college. They came from all over China to see Chairman Mao. How I envied them! One lad, just four years older than me, wore a badge from Shaoshan, Mao's birthplace. The Red Guards loved to pay pilgrimage trips to sacred revolutionary places such as Shaoshan, Jinggangshan, and Yenan. I made friends with him, and we swapped badges. Later, I exchanged more with the Red Guards who came and went. My collection had begun. My parents were my main source,

mostly free from their work units. I was really thick-skinned, asking their friends, colleagues and neighbors. "Little man, why do you want Mao badges?" they asked. "I love them and collect them." Yet I myself didn't understand quite why I was so fascinated. They were shiny, interesting and fun, and despite my youth, I did have deep affection for Chairman Mao, through education at school and home. Each new gain delighted me. I pinned them to large handkerchiefs and proudly showed them off to my friends, none of whom had so many. The badges produced by the army were generally better than civilian efforts. At first, I enjoyed wearing interesting badges that guaranteed attention in the street. Once, a nasty older boy snatched a new badge from my chest, which left me wailing for some time. Since then, I carefully kept my dear badges at home. Stealing happened from time to time, but it was not for money in those days. Mao badges were simply the most desirable item. (Zhang and MacLeod 1999:151)

In debating the bourgeois nature of badge collection and exchange, it is significant to note that badge exchanges rarely involved money. When they did, it was unacceptable to frame the transaction as buying and selling. Instead, proprietors and consumers used the phrase "to invite." Others report on the refusal to involve money in exchanges. According to Gao, vendors protested the notion of selling him a badge:

We are not speculators . . . we only trade. Two small ones for a big one. What if I did not have any badges to trade? "You can use Chairman Mao photos instead. Ten photos for one badge." I had seen youths on the sidewalk selling photos of Chairman Mao receiving the first group of Red Guards. A pack of ten cost eight mao,

which seemed rather expensive. But the idea of returning to Yizhen with a Chairman Mao badge captivated
me. . . . I ran off to find a photo dealer, came back with
two packs, and bartered them for two small badges. I
pinned one on my chest and the other inside my pocket.
I was sure I could feel Chairman Mao's radiance burning into me. (Gao 1987:120)

In his discussion of his use of badges to obtain transportation, Ling (1972:86) writes: "The drivers did not dare
openly ask for money from us for fear that we would take
down their license numbers and report them to the authorities. Instead, they asked for Mao badges, which they could
trade on the black market."

Ling's characterization of a black market in badges is
apt. Dai provides a vivid portrait of the ambience of badge
trading markets:

We noticed in the course of our travels that every city
manufactured its own badges, probably because local
power holders wished to express their total loyalty to
Mao Zedong: thus, it had been possible to distribute
one to each visiting student. Shanghai was no excep-
tion. But of even greater interest was the wide scale
exchange activity surrounding these souvenirs. Shanghai had two major "Mao badge trading markets," one
at the famous "Great World" and one at Shanghai's
North Railway Station. The general bustle and confusion in these two areas would be hard to exaggerate.
Our group found it impossible to stay together in the
surging crowd, and always arranged in advance a time
and place to meet to go home. Because it constituted a
serious traffic problem, policemen came along every
now and then to stop the trading. Whenever this happened, however, everyone hid their badges and told the

police they were "enjoying the crowd." Activity revived after the law left the scene. . . . One surviving remnant of Shanghai's history as a commercial city was its concentration of crafty businessmen. No small number of people over thirty years of age could be found walking through the markets, puffing out their chests to display all sorts of strange souvenir badges pinned on their jackets. Obviously they were in search of buyers. When we proposed trades, however, they just looked at us contemptuously; they wanted seven or eight of our badges in exchange for just one of theirs . . . . It was fashionable during the Cultural Revolution to wear Mao badges to express total loyalty to the Chairman. The demand from Red Guard collectors was so great, however (some people accumulated them like postage stamps), that workers, peasants, and government cadres were often not able to secure even one. Production was simply insufficient. Our friends back in Kwangtung were later willing to pay high prices for badges we had accumulated. (Bennett and Montaperto 1972:121)

Police raids of badge markets were common. Targeting the Mao trade as "disloyal," undercover officers would seize (and, often, pocket) badges during raids. One long-term badge collector hints at his use of guanxi as a former security officer in Beijing to collect vast quantities of badges:

During the Cultural Revolution, people like me who worked for the government offices went idle. We did not have much to do. That is how I had time to cultivate my interest in badges. Besides collecting badges, I also collected little journals published by the different fighting teams. I was not by myself while collecting all of these. Many people were collecting and exchanging badges. Of course, some people had better conditions to collect than others. I had guanxi with a couple of badge factories, so whenever they produced some badges they would give me a couple of them.

Zhou (1993) claims that Red Guards took advantage of such police raids, using their status as informal political aficionados to confiscate badges. Reports of badge theft were common during the Cultural Revolution. Zhou provides a colorful reiteration of the prevalence of badge theft. He claims that many mended shirts from the Cultural Revolution are evidence that badges were ripped off shirts. Zhou also suggests that badge robbery did not necessarily reflect ethical problems, citing the popularity of Lu Xun's philosophy that for one who loves to read, stealing books is not a crime.

Li (1993:11) describes the covert approach of traders at Beijing's Loyalty Station as they attempted to circumvent the insult of trading: "Most of these traders wore heavy coats. Inside the coats, they were wearing all kinds of Mao Zedong badges. When there was an exchange going on, people would unbutton their coats and show their collection to other people and do their business. When there was no deal going on, they would just button their coats, wander about, stroll around, pretending that nothing was happening. This was safe, convenient, and avoided a lot of suspicion."

In a short story, Feng depicts a similar scenario when the protagonist, Kong, approaches a dubious trader:

> The speaker was a big, tall middle-aged man with the unctuous manner of a practiced salesman. But he was wearing a baggy blue jacket with only a single bottlecap-sized Mao button on the chest. He did not look as though he had any special goods. "I want a big one. At least a three-and-a-half. Do you have any?" . . .

"First tell me what you have," the man replied without batting an eyelid. He was as haughty as a Mao-button millionaire. "I've got dozens of different kinds," said Kong, reaching for his pocket. The man touched Kong's wrist. "Don't take them out in this mob. Somebody will swipe them. Come with me!"

Following the trader to a back alley, Kong displayed his badges and challenged the trader to show whether or not he had any badges:

> Instead of answering, the man unfastened his outer jacket and whisked it open. Kong's eyes nearly popped out of his head: at least a hundred different Mao buttons were pinned to the man's inner jacket. He was a walking Mao-button treasure house. Kong had never seen any of the styles before. "You haven't seen anything yet," the man said before Kong could look his fill. "Take a peek inside—that's where the big ones are." And he opened the button-covered jacket to reveal yet another garment laden with row upon row of shiny buttons. They were huge: all were at least as big as a fist, and one, the size of the lid of a mug, caught the eye like a crane among chickens. (Feng 1985:19)

Gao remembers the very real dangers of black market badge exchange:

> In front of a department store by the Pearl River, we found a brisk night market in Chairman Mao badges. We held up packs of Chairman Mao photos and shouted: "Ten photos for one Jinggang Mountain badge! Ten photos for one Yenan badge!" Suddenly, we found ourselves surrounded by five youths who were wearing sunglasses even though it was dark. They snatched our photos, ripped them up, and scattered the pieces.

"Those are pictures of Chairman Mao!" I protested.
"How dare you tear them up! Counterrevolutionaries!"
One of them knocked me down with a punch to the
chest. . . . The buzz of bartering around us subsided for
a few moments, but nobody came to our assistance.
(Gao 1987:168)

The black market exchange of Mao badges and other
icons held such subversive potential that the government
ordered the end of such exchanges in a 1967 circular that
prohibited "all private selling or exchange of all types of
commemorative badges, placards bearing quotations, photographs, newspapers and other materials."

Guanxi

Appadurai's (1992) invitation to explore the calculative dimension of all things is particularly helpful in relation to research on Mao badges. Challenging the
anthropological tradition of romanticizing exchange in non-
industrialized societies as being pure or unfettered by the
vagaries of calculation and self-interest, Appadurai urges
anthropologists to understand the spirit of the commodity
in all cultures. This blurring between long static categories
of gift versus commodity exchange imbues the material
world with a multidimensionality previously untapped.

Mao badges clearly held a commodity potential that
hinted of an underground capitalism. However, a simple
interpretation of badge exchange as capitalist parody would
ignore the nature of Chinese reciprocity. Badge exchange
entailed an etiquette that more closely (and with equal irony)
resembled long-standing indigenous traditions of reciprocity, in particular the spirit of guanxi. At the most basic level,
guanxi refers to "social connections that enable a person to

negotiate the countless 'passes' or 'gates' thrown in his or her way" (M. Yang 1994:49). Guanxi is a multifaceted, sometimes contradictory, but always integral process of Chinese social exchange that conflates familiarity and trust, self-interest and instrumentality, and obligation and indebtedness (M. Yang 1994).

Native conceptualizations of guanxi identify an inherent sociability involving emotional sentiment and an informality opposed to official organization. Often misread as bribery, guanxi embodies a self-interest that guides exchanges without compromising the sociability of those exchanges. According to Mayfair Yang, guanxi is intrinsically opposed to official ambitions. Popular interpretations emphasize this element of social connections and exchange: "Guanxi stories provide narratives of people who can shape their own destinies and who can triumph even though they are weak. These stories also construct a sense of collective endeavor, of people relying on one another to outwit the system" (M. Yang 1994:56). In contrast, official renderings of guanxi characterize such relationships as self-cultivating, feudal, and antithetical to the communal socialist good.

The calculative nature of Mao badge exchange to obtain capital is congruous with the discernment of guanxi as uniquely sociable, subversive, and instrumental. Guanxi informed the exchange and consumption of Mao icons in ironic contrast to official dogma that prohibited the perpetuation of traditional, or feudalistic, forms of social interaction. It was the very introjection of politics into everyday life that served the manipulation of Mao propaganda to establish, rather than subvert, a ritualized comportment of self and social relationships. The sustenance of guanxi through badge exchange defies simplistic notions of a Maoist personality cult. Without doubt, Chinese citizens idolized Mao; however, Mao was as much a means to procure, manipulate, and dispute identity as he was an end in himself. The use of badges to shield and pursue various agendas during the Cultural Revolution accommodated the sustenance, or transformation, of traditional forms of social alliance. Though badges clearly bore material gain, their commodity potential lay equally with their ability to curry political capital, particularly in relation to the competitive consumption spurred by Red Guard enmity. Within the broader context of Chinese reciprocity, the exchange of Mao badges followed a normative etiquette of exchange with a political twist; in accumulating badges, individuals aspired toward the more abstract return of political capital, or "redness."

Instances of badge use in social exchanges during the Cultural Revolution reflect notions of guanxi as a scheme of networks of exchange organized to negotiate an official bureaucratic system. Badges offered a currency through which the Chinese public manipulated "the system" and circumvented official rhetoric. The use of Mao as a vehicle for state propaganda resulted in a circuitous consumption by which Chinese citizens had some opportunity to inflect the intended meanings of the state, inflections that reached a climax in the extreme factionalism that occurred during the Cultural Revolution. While this process distracted the cultivation of individual relationships, Mao exchange offered an avenue of mutual sociability by allowing a communal satisfaction in "beating the system." The state was not successful in obliterating social dynamics in Chinese society, because the messenger, Mao, was symbolically adaptable to citizens' desires, needs, and ideals. Chinese citizens creatively co-opted a strident national narrative by reconciling Mao propaganda with traditional, potentially subversive, legacies of exchange rooted in indigenous meanings of social relationships.

At the same time that Mao rituals permeated everyday

life, Chinese citizens manipulated Mao to challenge the political gates of the Cultural Revolution. If one accepts Mayfair Yang's (1994) premise that guanxi is inherently sociable and subversive, it is fair to suggest that a profound layer of sociability existed at some level during the Cultural Revolution. This sociability involved, to some extent, the establishment and maintenance of friendly exchanges within the traumatic disentanglement of social relationships. Yang further claims that guanxi reflects an "alternative subjectivity," where human nature enjoys the freedom of autonomous expression. Even in a time when the state exhibited an enormous amount of control over its citizens, political and material exchange accommodated a degree of power in circumventing the hegemonic forces of the central government. At the same time that Mao consumption was bound in a state-centered national narrative, it simultaneously offered the luxury of mediating that narrative, activating subjectivities that engaged and innovated state politics. The increased sophistication of maintaining and forging social networks during the Cultural Revolution resulted in a more informal and expansive social repertoire that would be summoned for the kaleidoscopic consumption ethic of post-Mao China.

6

The Red

Old Days

Heritage, Historical Memory, and the Endurance of Mao

Given the historical energy of the consumption of Mao's image, it is not surprising that Mao reappeared with a vengeance in the 1990s. His iconic re-emergence in contemporary China following the *Maore* (Mao craze) in the early 1990s raises interesting questions regarding the enduring potential of his image in relation to Chinese nationalism. Mao has not easily disappeared, and expunging his image—and the power associated with it—is politically charged. The co-optation of Mao and the Cultural Revolution in contemporary China reveals the ambiguity of China's present and future direction. The iconic revival of Mao in contemporary China is a multifaceted phenomenon, involving the resurgence of Mao's image as good luck charm, tourist commodity, political symbol, and avant-garde artistic expression. The myriad modern manifestations of Mao reflect an increasingly diversified career that speaks to a changed socioeconomic and increasingly transnational landscape.

In an age marked by financial and ideological exchanges between nations, little immunity is available to the increasingly porous boundaries in and between nations. As outlined in the introduction to this book, recent scholarship suggests that it is inappropriate to consider cultural consumption without reference to the transnationalism or globalization that characterizes the modern world. Hannerz (1989), for example, claims that these global interchanges result in increased sophistication in accessing and recontextualizing knowledge. Thus, research to some degree must acknowledge the probability that subjects are working with what Kearney (1995) terms "binational repertoires." Research also attends to the ways in which actors employ memory and present heritage in the global sphere (Anagnost 1997; Bruner 1996; Bruner and Kirshenblatt-Gimblett 1994; S. Errington 1998; F. Errington and Gewertz 1996; Kirshenblatt-Gimblett 1998; Lanfant et al. 1995; Linnekin 1992). The multiple invocations of Mao Zedong and the Cultural Revolution in contemporary China offer a provocative context to identify ways in which historical memories intersect with these "transnational interactions" (Hannerz 1989).

The historical memory that is presented in China today is as varied as the contexts in which Mao and the Cultural Revolution have reappeared. Consistent with other studies on the presentation of heritage, China's presentation of Mao and the Cultural Revolution reflect a selective memory. However, the notion of historical memory is too static to apply to China's contemporary encounter with its historical past. Analyzing China's current trafficking in Mao in terms of reinventing history is incomplete. The Mao phe-

nomenon in China today is not simply a display of historical memory, but is a national catharsis in which the Chinese are reenacting history with a great deal of innovation.
The contemporary Mao phenomenon is a theater of historical interchange in which the all-too-familiar process of "selective amnesia" (Schwarcz 1991) is as much an opportunity
to co-opt the Cultural Revolution as to remember, forget,
or reinvent it.

Melting Mao

Barmé (1996) discusses the Mao pulping process in
contemporary China in great depth, including a translation
of Central Department of Propaganda documents written
in 1978 relating to the correct management of the
Chairman's image. Though the document details everything
from Mao slogans to Mao statues, the party's decision on
"disposal of extant objects related to loyalty" is particularly
relevant:

> According to a report received from the general politi-
> cal department of the PLA dated 19 July, during the
> course of clearing out its warehouses the Army has
> come across large stocks of objects related to "loyalty."
> These include Mao statues made of aluminum, plas-
> ter of paris, porcelain and other materials, as well as
> badges. According to incomplete statistics from five
> departments in the Kunming military region alone,
> they have in excess of 2,300 kilograms of Chairman
> Mao badges, ten metal molds, 720 plastic statues of
> the Chairman, 100 plaster and porcelain statues, 250
> portraits on tinplate, 550 on plywood, as well as 6000
> quotation badges. Some of these are of inferior quality
> and the images thereon substandard, others have

warped or are soiled, some are half made, and a considerable number of them feature inscriptions by Lin
Biao. This is not merely an army matter, it is a problem that exists throughout the society at large. In order to dispose appropriately of statues and badges that
detract from the glorious image of Our Great Leader
and Teacher Chairman Mao, we suggest the following: 1. Units and organizations that have large stores
of badges, statues, embroidered images, paintings and
quotation badges similar to those described in the
above, regardless of whether they are fully or only par-
tially complete, should hand them over to their political departments for disposal. All objects that are: i.
Crudely made and substandard; ii. Are warped or dam-
aged; or, iii. Marked with inscriptions by Lin Biao, are
to be destroyed. The metal, paper and chemical materials remaining should be recycled by local factories.
In the case of porcelain and plaster works these should
be broken up and buried in suitable locations. 2. The
disposal of these statuettes and badges is an extremely
serious business. The relevant party committees involved should strengthen ideological and political work
during the disposal process and be sure to explain to
the workers involved in carrying out this task its ob-
jectives and frame of reference so as to avoid any mis-
understandings. (Barmé 1996:129)

The government remains ambiguous in its management
of Mao and the Cultural Revolution. Despite efforts to dispose of Mao icons, the government has found value in Mao's
image in anchoring some semblance of Communist ideology in a runaway economic system, yet it has gone to great
lengths to weaken the power of that image. For example,
the government produced seventy thousand "Deng badges"

marked with "China's Chief Architect" on front and "Socialism with Chinese Characteristics" (in Chinese and English) on the back. In 1995, these badges sold for about thirty-five yuan per badge. Manufacturers, however, have suggested that the badges not be worn; the gold plating rubs off and ruins their value (Sun-Childers 1995). In addition to his image on badges, Deng's fame was perpetuated through the Institute of Deng Xiaoping Theory in Tianjin (Terrill 1993). Mao's solitary slumber in the Mao mausoleum has also been disrupted with the installation of Zhou Enlai and Zhu De rooms (minus the bodies).

Grandchildren of the Cultural Revolution

Beginning in the 1990s, economic and political interests overrode official efforts to dispose of Mao icons. In many ways, Chinese youth who didn't experience the Cultural Revolution led the Mao revival when young intellectuals paraded his image during the 1989 pro-democracy movement, and only a minority sport Mao badges in China today. Scholars suggest that the youthful interest in Mao has been intensified by dissatisfaction with the current regime (Friedman 1994; Scharping 1994; Schram 1994; Watson 1991). The student-inspired Mao is typically limited to a young, pre–Cultural Revolution Mao. As was common during the Cultural Revolution, students in the pro-democracy movement of 1989 capitalized on symbolic languages, using animal imagery, broken bottles, and distinctive clothing, including headbands and T-shirts (Wasserstrom 1991). At the same time that Chinese youth posed a martyred Mao during the pro-democracy movement, protesters invoked memories of the Cultural Revolution toward negative ends. Students accused Deng Xiaoping of "errors of a gravity no less than those in the Cultural Revolution," while Deng accused students of "exposing China to the dangers of Maoism" (Young 1994:24). Young uses the concept of ancien régime, in which a demonized past rationalizes a golden future, to explain this Mao mudslinging.

Pro-democracy protesters enjoyed the power that Mao's image offered to resist the current government, yet contested perceptions of themselves as modern-day versions of the Red Guards. Students also defied perceptions of their exhibition of Mao as a naive cult revival by syncretizing his image with prerevolutionary and foreign elements. For example, student protesters used wall posters to air complaints, surrounded buildings to call on leaders, and employed stylistic devices meant to reach workers, all reminiscent of the historical May Fourth movement. To reach foreign audiences, student protesters downplayed patriotism while emphasizing democratic ideals and using foreign languages (Wasserstom 1991). The goddess of democracy provided the most striking entreaty to Western audiences. An ingenious "pastiche of imported and native symbolism," the goddess of democracy, in addition to tapping Western sentiment, served as an analogue to the Chinese past, suggestive of feudal Chinese gods, socialist realist statues, and the Mao statues of the Cultural Revolution (Esherick and Wasserstrom 1994).

Out of the Closet: Street Mao

Continued fascination with the power of the late Chairman's image dwarfs official efforts to manage Mao's material legacy. The *Maore* began in the 1980s and culminated on Mao's centenary. Though the Maore might have peaked in 1993, the consumption of Mao icons extends well into the present day. Mao badges flood Chinese antique markets; badge collectors open museums; and Cultural Revolution theme restaurants become increasingly popular.

Mao's image proliferates in resourceful ways: it is pasted on lighters, lockets, T-shirts, tie clips, lamps, telephone cards, knives, alarm clocks, cigarette packs, and yo-yos, to name a few. While these trinkets were relatively low in price in 1995, a few companies have experimented with upping the stakes for Mao's image. For example, a Mao statue was auctioned internationally, starting at one million dollars (W. Chan 1994). A Shanghai company reported selling out of diamond-studded Mao watches priced at approximately six thousand yuan (1200 dollars), and, in 1991, a pop rendition of Cultural Revolution lyrics called "The Red Sun" reportedly sold six million copies in less than twelve months.

This frivolity with Mao's image borders mockery, particularly in the use of Mao in avant-garde art. For example, the international exhibition "Mao goes pop" included a clown-faced Mao, Mao with daisies, and pastel Maos; a collection of Chinese avant-garde art also featured a variety of surreal Maos (Noth 1991). A Canton nightclub singer, Hua Gong, performed a version of the famous 1960s song "I Love Beijing Tiananmen" to amused crowds. A Chinese Christmas celebration at a Beijing nightclub in 1993 found Chinese and foreigners dancing to rock music intermingled with the "East is Red"; the Christmas tree was decorated with Mao ornaments, and Mao was flashed spastically on screen to the Clash's "Should I Stay or Should I Go." Jeering Mao was not uncommon in everyday discourse among the Chinese, as is evident by the many Mao jokes spread in China following his death. One such joke recently surfaced on the Internet. The author, a Chinese student, writes in true transnational style, conflating Li Zhisui's tell-all memoir about Mao, Chinese history, and the political intrigues of President Clinton:

> When President Clinton read Mao's former doctor's memoir, he wondered how Mao could get away with many of his romances. With the help of an astrologer, he met Mao in the afterworld.

Mao:	This is the second time I have received an American President.
Clinton:	It is a great glory to be received by you. I will report back to my people.
Mao:	You must have come to me for something.
Clinton:	To tell you the truth, I am being sued for two allegations.
Mao:	What the hell are they?
Clinton:	One is sex harassment. The other is an extramarital affair.
Mao:	What is sixth harassment? You developed my tactics for guerilla warfare?
Clinton:	Sex, not sixth, the sex of man and woman. Sex harassment means playing with a girl you are not supposed to.
Mao:	You are young and at the peak of your sexual prosperity. Even the old man in the Dream of the Red Chamber stole his daughter-in-law. You got someone laid?
Clinton:	Nobody but the intern in my office. That chick! My mouth waters whenever I think of her.
Mao:	What the hell! I got my secretary laid for years and no one passed a wind! Seems some people want to topple you. You confessed?
Clinton:	No, I would be done for if I confessed.
Mao (smile):	I like rightists. Rightists tell the truth. You are bad. You do not tell the truth.
Clinton:	Your Chairman, could you please give me some tips since you never got caught in bed with someone?

Mao: You just do it! Build a small room adjacent to your duck egg office. You work hard. Even if you achieve nothing, you deserve it for having worked.

Clinton: How do I explain to my people?

Mao: You explain shit! You are having a rest. It is nothing embarrassing. You do it in broad daylight, not in the dark.

Clinton: Media is a headache.

Mao: You should have your media. Set up your cannon to bombard the headquarters of those who conspire against you. If you cannot do it in Washington, you just go down south. You should know how to set up another government. Even a rabbit has three homes! Your hometown will do. You have half of America behind you if you go into guerrilla warfare. I had a cave in my hometown.

Clinton: What about my wife?

Mao: Even a shrew shows her fangs occasionally. You just give her some work to do and she will not think of you. I gave my wife eight Beijing operas to deal with and I was free during the Cultural Revolution. Say, I hear your wife is pretty. Does she dance? [According to Li's memoir, Mao used dancing in the 1960s to court young women.]

Mao's image also resurfaced as a good-luck symbol in taxis. The windshield Maos are rumored to shield passengers from chaotic city traffic and, in the countryside, to bar them against flooding and other natural disasters. One respondent, discussing Mao's mysterious nature, attempted to prove his case with a popularly circulated story. He said that bad weather followed the defacement of Mao's portrait in Tiananmen Square during the pro-democracy movement, but when the portrait was restored, the bad weather subsided. Furthermore, he claimed that flowers bloomed in the middle of winter in Shaoshan upon the unveiling of a Mao statue. He admitted that while he was not superstitious, he did wonder about the Shaoshan story.

Probably the most famous site of revolutionary devotion, Shaoshan continues to memorialize Mao with an undeniably capitalist edge. The Shaoshan Statue Factory sells thousands of Mao busts and name cards with Mao's quotation, "A bright future is ahead." In 1993, a new thirty-three-foot Mao statue was built, and one million dollars was invested in Mao's exhibition hall. Tang Ruiren, the wealthy owner of the Mao Family Restaurant, only accepted "donations" for meals at first. But now: "In his day I didn't want to own a restaurant, but today I want it to make sure that people eat well. In this way I can help China's development. Long live Chairman Mao!" (Schmetzer 1993:5). Her son, also a restaurant owner in Beijing, serves the people similarly: "As Chairman Mao used to say, 'People must have a better life'" (Schmetzer 1993:6). In addition to the host of Mao souvenir stands in Shaoshan, residents capitalize on their geographical link to Mao, recalling stories about his early life, particularly as they manufacture "important sites" to tour in Shaoshan. The village boasts a wealth of Mao surnames, and hosts are generous with their genealogies, transforming Mao's family tree into an overgrown weed.

Contemporary Badge Markets

In contemporary China, Cultural Revolution badges exist in abundance in antique and street markets. These badges range in price and reflect the variety of themes, styles, and materials that emerged during the Cultural Revolution. When I visited street markets in Beijing in 1995, most vendors included some type of Mao paraphernalia in their repertoire; in fact, it was quite common for Mao badges and Little Red Books to be advertised in display windows. In Liulichang antique market—a pricey shopping area dressed up as an old Chinese village that caters to foreign tourists—

vendors maintained a healthy market for Mao badges, Mao busts, and Little Red Books. At Liulichang, badges typically sold for 15 yuan (3 dollars) per badge, while Mao busts averaged 80 yuan (16 dollars). When asked how they determined badge prices, the majority of vendors responded that size was the primary factor. The third floor of Hongqiao Market offers the second major attraction in Beijing for Mao memorabilia (among other things). Here, badge prices ranged from 300 to 500 yuan (60 to 100 dollars). Hongqiao also included a large number of statues featuring Lin Biao and Mao Zedong, priced at about 350 yuan (70 dollars). At one stand, a clock with both Mao and Deng Xiaoping sold for 700 yuan (140 dollars). Again, vendors repeatedly rationalized price differences by virtue of the size of the badges. Though Chinese regularly frequented Hongqiao Market, it was Westerners who typically zeroed in on the Mao relics.

While badge exchange was prominent during the Cultural Revolution, the nature of exchange in contemporary China is unapologetically capitalist. Badge exchange in contemporary China is not couched in politically correct barter and gift cycles as during the Cultural Revolution. Badges are commodities that are openly bought and sold with money in the new free-market system. This traffic in Mao's image is only vaguely reminiscent of the widespread propagation of his image during the Cultural Revolution. The Chinese are reliving the zealous circulation of his image with a playful sacrilege strictly forbidden during the Cultural Revolution. Mao has been remystified as he becomes a consumer item and the antithesis of what was acceptable in the art world during the Cultural Revolution. Chinese people are increasingly becoming aware of the economic value of Mao icons due to the publicity surrounding contemporary badge collectors. Take, for example, the following ad from a Hunan collector:

Cash for your Chairman Mao badges! There are many Chairman Mao badges gathered around that, for different reasons, have not been discovered and used properly. With the passing of time, their value is increasing. They have caused great attention among both domestic and international antique collectors. If you spend some time collecting these badges you are sure to make a fortune. If you want to collect badges, you can use your spare time, and without much energy, you can make a lot of money. Everybody has Cultural Revolution badges. Many have not realized their value. Whoever starts collecting first will be sure to become rich. We now offer cash for whatever kinds of Chairman Mao badges that you have. As soon as we receive your badge, we will send you cash. As long as you exchange with us according to the following regulations and pricing, we assure your fortunes. (Zhou 1993)

The re-creation of Mao badges has not been without some ambivalence, however, as illustrated in the following excerpt written to an advice columnist in a current-affairs magazine:

There is an arts and crafts factory in our district. According to reliable information, they want to produce a certain amount of Mao Zedong badges, but they're not sure if it is feasible. Some say this is not compatible with current party policies, some say it is a good thing because every Chinese misses Chairman Mao and a badge can express this sentiment. The answers the factory got from the local business management department and the relevant governmental offices is also very blurry. So they came to us, the public security bureau for relevant regulations, which we have no knowledge of either.

The advisers responded:

> Comrade, there are two aspects to this question. One
> concerns the production and management. Regarding
> whether they can produce badges, I haven't personally
> come across regulations restricting or permitting the
> production of Mao Zedong badges or similar arts and
> crafts products. However, this can also be a political
> and social issue. I think that the whole party and all
> the people love Mao Zedong. However, to express our
> love and respect to Mao, we don't necessarily have to
> wear or produce Chairman Mao badges. We have to
> learn from the lessons of the Cultural Revolution. It is
> now high time that we practice and promote Maoism
> with our behavior and practice instead of formality.
> (Zhou 1993)

In a narrative describing his attempt to obtain a heart-
shaped, hand-carved ivory badge, Zhou illustrates the awk-
wardness of contextualizing his post-Mao collecting activity
with a market economy:

> Suppressing my excitement, I asked the man at the
> booth if he would sell the badge. The guy swiped it
> back and stuck it up. He was not happy I had touched
> his precious badge. I hung around his stand for quite a
> while thinking it would only make it worse if I in-
> sisted. I knew he'd be around the next day, so I returned,
> pretending nothing had happened. I bought several
> small items, then I picked up the piece of ivory badge
> to appreciate it. This time I was very careful. I asked,
> "Should I invite this badge at this time," and I empha-
> sized the word invite. He recognized me from the day
> before and was not happy. He said to me, "No invita-
> tion, no invitation," and drove me away. Upon hearing

this, I was almost desperate and could not respond for quite a while. After two sleepless nights, I changed my wardrobe and borrowed a pair of glasses. With this costume on, I came to the old man's stand again. This time I bought some useless items, socks, buttons, spending more than ten yuan. The old man was very pleased and carefully wrapped my purchase with newspaper. I started my new attack again. I almost whispered to him, "I would like to invite this Chairman Mao badge again; how much renmenbi do you want?" Again, I emphasized the character invite, but the three characters, renmenbi, felt kind of awkward, because I'd never said them with "invite" before. The old man studied me carefully, looking like a judge. I was thoroughly embarrassed. Holding my package in the air, he seemed to be remembering something. I felt like a thief at this moment and was afraid he would recognize who I was. So I decided to tell the truth after all. I took off the glasses and told him my intentions. I told him I wanted the badge for my collection. My sincerity eventually knocked open the old man's door. After hearing my explanation, he laughed. He said he had kept the badge for very long and did not really want to give it up, but that since I liked it so much he would give it to me as a gift. I felt very lucky. . . . Before I left, I took all the money from my pocket and gave it to him. The old man was irritated and said, "Haven't you already paid me?" He was referring to all the stuff I had bought in the past few days. He handed the money back to me. That night I slept soundly and had good dreams.

Contemporary Badge Collectors

Though Mao badge collecting was extensive during the Cultural Revolution, recent efforts have been made to professionalize collecting through the establishment of exhibitions, museums, publications, and associations—all of which aim to distinguish professional collectors. Collectors delineate the terms for professionalism as related to both quantity and quality, often commenting on the desire among these professionals to disassociate themselves from the traffic in Mao badges that flourishes in China today. Professional collections should surpass five thousand in number without replicas based on the estimate that fifty thousand different types of badges were created during the Cultural Revolution; professionals must attain at least 10 percent. Quality, however, is more important than quantity; 8 percent of the collection should reflect middle- to upper-grade badges. The collection should also contain "special" badges that might include pre–Cultural Revolution badges, single existing piece badges, rare badges (via theme or material), and set, pair, and series badges. For example, one collector boasts the wide-ranging geographical and historical coverage of his collection that embodies single, set, and series badges. The collection includes pieces from every province in China and documents a wide range of political, economic, and cultural events from 1949 to the 1990s. His comprehensive coverage extends to badge materials, including gold, silver, bronze, stainless steel, tin plate, optical glass, bone, gemstone, marble, plaster, and stone. The most unique badge in his collection is allegedly the largest badge in the world, a mammoth wall-mounted Mao weighing over thirty-eight pounds and measuring one hundred and twenty centimeters in diameter.

Another collector remembers his disillusionment in competing with the extensive nature of other collections.

He almost quit collecting until a friend advised him to find and master his own niche. He now claims the most extensive Mao statue collection in China. Another collector boasts about the quality rather than quantity of his collection in an almost accusatory tone: "With some inferior quality badges you cannot really see Chairman Mao's eyes. It looks like he's wearing glasses."

In addition to focusing on quantity and quality, a more obscure criterion for professional collectors is that they must claim higher ambitions than simply collecting; their collections should be accompanied by knowledge about badge history or esthetics to be shared through exhibitions and research. In a farewell letter, a long-time retiring collector encouraged the increased professionalization of badge collecting, condemning the chaos of the collecting field, denouncing collectors selling "fake" relics, or reproductions, and relics of inferior quality. He also condemns irresponsible boasting and historical inaccuracy concerning badges. He calls upon collectors to reexamine their moral standards, emphasizing that collecting is not for entertainment or profit. He recommends a national organization that pursues more systematic collecting.

The self-presentation of professional collectors reeks of values reminiscent of the Cultural Revolution: self-sacrifice, endurance, suffering, and service to the people. This is best exemplified by Wang Anting of Chengdu, who is perhaps the most famous collector. Wang was the first to start a museum and research association—all in his one-room home. His Mao badge collection exceeds fifty thousand badges. He emphasizes his proletarian background as a carpenter, a trade he used during the Cultural Revolution to increase his collection of badges. He explains his twenty years of collecting Mao memorabilia in terms of his devotion to Mao: "I'm one with Mao. . . . You should remember the person who dug the well to give you the water you're drinking" (Lubman 1991).

Wang's discussion of his ambitions is replete with altruism:

> I don't have anything with me now except Mao Zedong badges. I feel sorry that I don't have better conditions to find a peaceful place for Chairman Mao. All I expect from the society is understanding and support and with the help of everybody, we can build a clean and spacious exhibition hall for Chairman Mao, so that these Mao Zedong badges and all the Cultural Revolution materials can escape the poor conditions like mine, so that they can play a more active and positive role. (Li 1993:80)

In addition to his desire to collect a badge for every mile of the Long March, Wang sings a Cultural Revolution song to Mao every morning and has arranged his home as a museum of inspiration as much as presentation. He has even flanked his bed with Mao material so he can emerge from slumber under the eye of the great helmsman. Li describes the scene:

> The situation inside the house was astonishing, breathtaking. Everywhere in the room on the walls are glass frames in which Mao badges are kept. Under the frames were exhibition cabinets. In the center of the room there were more exhibition cabinets in which other Mao badges were kept and exhibited. On the cabinet, there are Mao statues. On the inside walls of the room, there are also different kinds of embroidered Mao pictures. Mao Zedong is everywhere in that house. Besides the different kinds of Mao portraits, there are a couple of wooden chairs and nothing else. Standing in

that room definitely made people recall the red ocean during the Cultural Revolution. (Li 1993:81)

Wang's proudest testimony to his selfless motivations is his refusal to sell his collection despite two healthy offers: American visitors offered fifty thousand dollars, and the Chinese Museum of History offered a new apartment (Sun-Childers 1995). Other collectors commonly point to their resistance to selling their badges as proof of their virtue and dismiss collectors willing to commercialize their badges. The virtue collectors associate with their activities serves to legitimate their status as collectors and distinguish their collections, as is evident in Ma's explanation of his collecting activities:

> I resumed my hobby in 1991, almost by accident, after a colleague showed off a large Mao badge. "You collect all sorts of things, why not Mao badges?" I had been collecting matchbox covers and key rings for a while. From a collector's point of view, Mao badges were produced in great volume and variety during the Cultural Revolution. As this was recent history, there would be many materials to aid my research. Inspired by his words, childhood memories flooded my mind. Excitedly, I went straight to my parents' house to look for my old collection. To my amazement, my father produced six hundred badges, including my own, carefully wrapped in foam. Holding my new-found wealth, I was almost dizzy with happiness! Only then did I realize my parents were collectors too. "During all these years, why didn't you throw them away?" "How could I?" my father replied. "I even took them into exile at a May Seventh cadre school in the countryside. These badges reflected my feelings towards Mao. Without him, a poor peasant boy like me might have died a

long time ago. These badges are works of art too." Although my father was attacked during the Cultural Revolution, that didn't change his love for Mao. He accepted the official verdict on Mao: 70 percent right and 30 percent wrong. That sums up my attitude too. Encouraged by my success, I launched a collecting campaign. I jumped when my mother-in-law said, "Oh, I just sold twenty kilograms of badges for scrap metal!" I had high expectations, as my father-in-law was once director of the Chairman Mao badge office under the army's railway division. Luckily, they kept the most attractive one hundred badges. I was just as thick-skinned as a child, asking everyone for badges. I am a sociable sort of chap with many friends, and within two years amassed over eleven thousand badges. Was I busy in those days. . . . In the years after the Cultural Revolution, badge values crashed: a few kilograms sold for one yuan at recycling stations. Some people threw them away, while others deliberately destroyed them, particularly those who had suffered badly. The government then demanded badges be returned for melting down. About half disappeared this way, while the rest circulate among the ordinary people. Over the past decade, Mao badges entered the market as revolutionary antiques and have become the third favorite after stamps and coins. Some people, who merely happen to have many badges at home, I wouldn't call real collectors, and I look down on those who collect for commercial reasons; some collect to remember that special period of history and others purely out of love for Mao. As for myself, my love for Mao is the sole motive for collecting and researching his badges. I wouldn't have been a collector for so long without loving the man. He founded a new China which was a much, much better place than the old, feudal China. Without him, the victory for the Chinese Revolution might have come much later. All Chinese have reason to be grateful to him, though, as a human being, he made mistakes too. Since he was a great man with great influence, his mistakes were also great, like the Cultural Revolution. Yet we should not totally deny Chairman Mao because of those mistakes. The search for hidden knowledge sustains my fascination for collecting. The creation of Mao badges during the Cultural Revolution took place in such a spontaneous and chaotic fashion that there is no proper record of these badges at all. One day I dearly hope to publish a comprehensive book with pictures of the badges and sound knowledge about them. I am obsessed with my badges. My son grew up hearing metal badges clinking together. Once I sat down to watch TV instead, but he couldn't sleep without the sound, until I pretended to play with the badges as usual. I clean them, polish them, sort and study different designs and back inscriptions, year of production, by whom, for what purpose and belonging to which set. My eyes become fixed on them, and apart from the badges in front of me, the whole world does not exist for me anymore. (Zhang and MacLeod 1999:152)

Not all individuals, however, maintain the righteous standards set by collectors. Many embrace the commodification of Mao, placing extravagant price tags on their piece of cultural heritage. Take, for example, the following advertisement of a Shenyang collector:

I am a member of the Association of Chinese collectors. During the Cultural Revolution, I began to collect cultural relics—badges with Mao Zedong's likeness. These badges were made during the Cultural Revolution from

1966 to 1976 throughout the whole country. The production was stopped after the Cultural Revolution.
Fewer and fewer badges have been kept during the last
thirty years, so they possess a very high collection
value. For the past nineteen years, I have collected fifty
thousand Mao Zedong badges with twenty thousand
varieties. I collected Mao Zedong badges of Jingde town
porcelain series. They were designed and made in 1969
for the purpose of greeting the Ninth National Conference of the Communist Party. The diameter of the biggest one is eighteen centimeters. The diameter of the
middle-sized one is eleven centimeters, and the diameter of the others is about five centimeters. The diameter of the smallest one is 0.8 centimeters which was
found to be the smallest badge made during the Cultural Revolution and was declared as the Guinness
world record. My collection of Mao Zedong badges
ranks among the highest in both quantity and variety
in the world. Now, I want to transfer my collections
or exhibit them to the world. I will transfer all fifty
thousand badges at the price of 100,000 U.S. dollars or
I will exhibit them in foreign museums, tourist spots
and large hotels.

This alleged revolutionary sanctuary of professional
collecting, despite its allegiance to the "real" Mao, has taken
more subtle liberties with the memory of the Cultural Revolution. The conspicuous consumption of professional
collections is moderately incompatible with Cultural Revolution notions regarding cultivation of the bourgeois. For
the mass markets, reliving the revolution is buffered by
Deng's free-market system; for professional collectors, reliving the revolution is softened by the comforts of display,
value, and prestige.

Recycling Mao

Badge collectors bemoan the ignorance among China's youth about the Cultural Revolution and official attempts to erase it from China's national memory. Efforts to forget the Cultural Revolution were readily apparent in Shenyang. One day, a Western friend told us that a local library planned to spend the afternoon pulping military and Red Guard magazines from the Cultural Revolution. We hurried to the library and negotiated with officials to give us the magazines. They were reluctant and annoyed but finally agreed to let us fill our duffel bags while they worked. They would not slow the progress of their pulping; we would have to grab what we could before they got to it. With little time to discriminate, we stuffed our bags, bicycled home, unloaded and returned to get more.

In more dramatic flair, Zhou (1992) recounts his own confrontations with badge recyclers in an attempt to save a rare set of badges from the furnace.

> There are several Sichuan blacksmiths making aluminum pots and pans for their customers. The red furnace fire and the hot scene attracted a lot of passersby. I was passing by and, driven by curiosity, joined the group. Next to the burning furnace along the heap of waste aluminum, I saw a pile of badges of all sizes among which there were nine pieces of nine centimeter diameter badges that caught my attention. This was really an unusual discovery for a collector like me. I rushed to the furnace and picked up the badges. I studied them each as an archeologist would an archeological site. What was more unusual was that these badges were exactly the badges I had been looking for for many years. They were made by an aviation military factory out of airplane parts by special technique. An old tech-

nician told me that these badges were not produced in large quantity and are of very high artistic value. I thought to myself, "Where there is a will, there is a way." In no time, the blacksmith started to put the waste material into the furnace and asked me to stand by. I said to the blacksmith, "Could you sell this waste aluminum to me? You can ask me for a lot of money." The blacksmith responded that these materials did not belong to them; they were brought by a local resident to process into aluminum pots and pans. They only took a processing fee and did not know where the residents lived or their names. The situation was complicated. The blacksmith insisted on throwing the badges into the furnace. Obviously, they felt that I was intruding with their processing, and they almost got into a quarrel with me. After some negotiations, I offered twice the processing fee (twelve yuan) so they would keep the badges until the owner came, so I could negotiate with the owner. I sat next to the furnace all day, not even going to buy lunch, even though I was starving. The owner of the badges did not come until afternoon rush hour. He was very angry when he saw his badges still there, not yet turned into an aluminum pot. He asked the blacksmith why he did not keep his word. I was very embarrassed and awkwardly started to explain the reason to him. I told him, "If you want an aluminum pot, I can go to the store and get a new one for you in exchange for the badges." That person saw through my anxiety, my desire for these badges and suddenly felt very nostalgic about the badges. He shook his head and said, "No exchange, no exchange. I will keep these to sell as cultural relics." He was very arrogant. I stood by the furnace for quite a while which moved the blacksmiths and several customers. They helped me convince the guy, and we finally reached a contract. I then had to pay more than thirty yuan for a new aluminum pot. A new aluminum pot for those dozen badges. It was turning late, and I was starting to feel very hungry, but I had no money to take the bus home. Badges in hand, I walked sixteen li and arrived home at midnight. My wife was very anxious and thought I had gotten into an accident.

Badge collectors insist on the educational component of badges and lobby for badges to be labeled as cultural relics. Collectors often frame their collections and exhibitions as de facto Cultural Revolution museums. Wang Anting, for example, houses his collection under the name "Wang Anting's Very Small Museum." In an interview with Dutton, Wang describes the process of trying to get an official license for the museum:

> When I had decided to set up the private museum, I went off to various government ministries to get permission and support. I went to the tax department and the cultural department but, instead of support, all I ended up getting was a lot of trouble and many hassles. Despite this, I still felt the need to continue with my plans. So I continued to work toward the opening of the exhibition. It was in this way that I ended up being the person to open up the first ever Mao Zedong badge exhibition. After it opened, lots of people came to see it and, although I charged an entrance fee, I decided not to charge students, the old or the crippled. People from the U.S., Germany, and Australia have all been to have a look. Also, Sichuan television has featured it in a report. The government, however, offered no subsidies and no support, although, in the end, they did give us help to repair the wall in the second room. They

also gave me this wheelchair. Generally, though, money comes from the donations of the people who visit. From this money I have now been able to put together a newsletter. My newsletter is called Contemporary Cultural Relic. I run off about two thousand copies of every edition. I think of Contemporary Cultural Relic as being like an underground newspaper that the CCP used to get its message across in pre-revolutionary days. (Dutton 1998:254)

Zhou earnestly outlines the case for badges as historical artifacts:

As the relics of an historical period, the value of Mao badges is by no means simply limited to their being craft objects. They are significant in that they embody the political, economic, and cultural values of the Cultural Revolution as a whole. In article two of the general provisions of the "Law of the People's Republic of China on the Protection of Cultural Relics" adopted at the twenty-fifth meeting of the standing committee of the fifth national people's congress on 19 November 1982, it stipulates that, "The state shall place under its protection, within the boundaries of the People's Republic of China, the following cultural relics of historical, artistic or scientific value: 1. Sites of ancient culture, ancient tombs, ancient architectural structures, cave temples, and stone carvings that are of historical, artistic or scientific value; 2. Buildings, memorial sites, and memorial objects related to major historical events, revolutionary movements or famous people that are highly memorable or are of great significance for education or for the preservation of historical data; 3. Valuable works of art and handicraft articles dating from various historical periods;

4. Important revolutionary documents as well as manuscripts and ancient or old books and materials, etc. that are of historical, artistic or scientific value; and 5. Typical material objects reflecting the social system, social production or the life of various nationalities in different historical periods." According to the detailed rules governing the legal determination of cultural relics, and in light of China's particular national situation, as well as in consideration of the three standards for apprising the status of relics (that is, that they are of historical, cultural, and scientific value), Mao badges should be considered as relics. They are of historical, artistic, and scientific value; will not be produced again; and, they are typical material objects with a unique appearance and are a direct and concrete representation of an historical reality. 1. Mao badges are the product of the Cultural Revolution, a major historical event and political movement. They are directly related to the ideology of the time, as well as the superstructure and the everyday lives of the Chinese people. On top of this, they have a unique value in that they commemorate a great man, Mao Zedong. At the same time, they constitute an "historical document" and are a means for the study of contemporary Chinese history and the Cultural Revolution. They are a firsthand record of the various incidents that occurred at the time. Mao badges are also representative works of contemporary Chinese industrial design that were produced using modern scientific methods and materials. They are typical of the then level of industrial design which is reflected in their range, immense number, and high quality. Without doubt they have significant historical, artistic and scientific value. 2. On 12 June 1969, party central issued a document, "Concerning

Certain Questions Deserving Consideration in Propagating the Image of Chairman Mao," which clearly stipulated that: "No further Chairman Mao badges are to be produced without the express authorization of the Centre." The circulation of this document marked the beginning of the end of the mass production of Mao badges. In the "CPC Party Central Directive on Questions related to Pursuing the Policy on Cutting back on Propagating Individuals" of 30 July 1980, a further advance was made on this when it stated that: "Chairman Mao badges are to be recalled and recycled wherever possible so as to prevent the excessive waste of metal." Following this, a nation-wide "cleaning out" and "handing over" of Mao badges was carried out in cities, the countryside, government organizations, factories, mines, companies, and the army all in the name of wiping out the negative influence of the "personality cult" and "contemporary superstition." Based on the writer's own observations and estimates made over a period of many years, this purge resulted in ninety percent of Mao badges being recycled, lost or destroyed, leaving a mere ten percent of the original number in circulation. That is to say, of the 4.8 billion Mao Zedong badges produced in the first years of the Cultural Revolution (1966–70), fewer than five hundred million are still extant. History has proved that the forms of commemoration related to Chairman Mao common during the Cultural Revolution, including the production of Mao badges, put too great an emphasis on the historical role of one individual. This resulted not only in considerable waste, but inferred that great men make history, something that was in direct conflict with Chairman Mao's statement that "the people create history." It is for this reason that Mao badges will not be produced in the future (although some badges have recently been manufactured for the Mao centenary, but their nature and significance is quite different from those made in the past). 3. Mao badges have a unique material quality. They are the concrete and physical embodiment of the political, economic, and cultural state, as well as of the social realities and spiritual mien of the people during the Cultural Revolution. They give people a physical sense—both visual and tactile—of an historical phenomenon. Mao badges circulated widely and in great numbers. They were highly-crafted products made from numerous different materials, the result of both traditional craftsmanship and modern industrial design. They melded sculpture, painting, calligraphy, and design to produce something elemental and representative in Easter art: works strong in imagery. Most Mao badges carry a portrait of Chairman Mao in relief with an effulgent red sun in the background. But many others represent Mao at various stages in his life with images of revolutionary holy places or maps of revolutionary significance in the background. They provide a true and powerful record of Comrade Mao's outstanding achievements in relation to the Chinese revolution, as well as depicting numerous major historical incidents. They are of great value for the study of Mao Zedong thought, party history, and the revolution. They can be used as visual aids in carrying out education concerning the traditions of the Chinese revolution and patriotic education. Moreover, on the back of many badges details of the place and date of various incidents of historical significance that occurred during the Cultural Revolution can be found. "The past is the teacher of the future." These details

can fill in other documents, as well as play an educa-
tive role for the young. (Barmé 1996:201)

Though Zhou is undoubtedly prone to some exaggera-
tion in his evaluation of badges, his discussion raises questions about the place of Mao badges in Chinese history. Of
course, the issue of Mao badges rests on the much larger
debate surrounding a Cultural Revolution museum, an issue first addressed publicly by Ba Jin, whose essay, "A Cultural Revolution Museum," is excerpted below.

In one of my random thoughts essays written some
time ago I recorded a conversation with a friend. In it I
suggested that they should build a Cultural Revolution museum. . . . I am sure few of those who were
baptised in the blood and fire of the Cultural Revolution will wish to remain silent. Everyone has his own
story to tell. One thing is certain: no one will make
out that the "cow sheds" were "heaven," or say that
the violent and ruthless murders that took place were
really part of a "Great Proletarian Cultural Revolution." People may have differences of opinion, but I
am sure we are of the same basic mind: none of us
wish to see another Cultural Revolution in China.
Another disaster that would mean the destruction of
our nation. I don't think I am being alarmist when I
say this. Everything that happened twenty years ago is
still clearly before my mind's eye. Those endlessly long
and painful days, the degradation and torture that so
many were put through, the distortions, deceptions,
confusion of good and bad, true and false, and all the
frame-ups, the endless injustices. You cannot tell me
we should forget all about it, or forbid people to talk

about it? That would only make it possible for another
Cultural Revolution to take place in twenty years time.
By then people would somehow think it was something new. . . . It is not that I do not want to forget; it is
simply that the gory spectre of the past has me in its
grip and will not let me go. How I let myself be dis-
armed, how the disaster crept up on me, just how that
tragedy unfolded, and the hateful role that I played in
it all, walked step by step towards an abyss. It is as
though it were all only yesterday. But I survived, even
though I was left a shell of a man. . . . "It will never be
repeated. Dry your tears and look to the future," my
friends urge, soothe me. But I remain only half convinced, and think to myself: we must wait and see.
And I did wait, right up to the time they started calling for "the elimination of spiritual pollution." I was
in the hospital at the time. . . . Every day the radio
would broadcast speeches by various provincial leaders denouncing "spiritual pollution." At night artists
and writers would appear on television and pledge
themselves to the fight to wipe out spiritual pollution.
On the surface I remained calm and collected, but when
I returned to the room each night I was haunted by
visions of those early days of the Cultural Revolution
in 1966. . . . After a year of reflection and analysis I
came to realize that neither the soil nor the climate
existed for a second Cultural Revolution. . . . The building of a Cultural Revolution museum is not the responsibility of one person. Everyone owes it to their
children and the future to leave a monument to the
harrowing lessons of the past. "Do not let history repeat itself" should not be an empty statement. Everyone must be made to see clearly, to remember fully.
That is why it would be best to build a museum, one

in which concrete and real things could be collected, emblems of the terrifying events of the Cultural Revolution, displayed so that people can see what actually happened here in China twenty years ago. Let people be confronted with the whole process and meditate on what we Chinese did throughout that decade. Force people to take off their masks, to show their conscience and to face themselves as they really are. Let them repay the debts of the past. Those who are not selfish will not be scared of being deceived, those who dare speak the truth will not easily fall for lies. Only by remaining mindful of the Cultural Revolution will people be able to prevent history from replaying itself. It is extremely important that we build this museum, for only by remembering the past can we be masters of the future. (Barmé 1999:381)

To substantiate his defense of Mao badges as cultural relics, Zhou refers to Ba Jin's essay and muses about the possibilities of a Cultural Revolution museum established by Ye Yonglie. In his urgency to validate badges, Zhou reproduces Ye's "response" to Ba's essay without indication of its fictional (and, seemingly, parodic) nature:

1. It was agreed that Ba Jin's essay "A Cultural Revolution Museum" summed up the aims and purposes of the museum; 2. Everyone who had submitted a plan felt that the museum should be in Beijing; 3. There were conflicting opinions as to whether the museum should be red, black or white. Those in favor of red argued that during the Cultural Revolution people talked of turning the world into a "sea of red." Others favored black as a color that represented the massive disaster of the period. Those who proposed white said it was to symbolize remembrance of those who died

in the holocaust. There were three proposals concerning the main entrance: 1. That a massive block of marble be set up engraved with Ba Jin's essay in gold. 2. That a stone bearing the inscription "16 May 1966– 6 October 1976, an unprecedented holocaust in Chinese history"; 3. That sixteen sculpted heads representing the sixteen ringleaders of the Lin Biao and Jiang Qing counter-revolutionary cliques be placed on a pillar of eternal shame. . . . The plans called for three exhibition halls. The Cultural Revolution was a period that revealed people's souls, therefore, the most important exhibit would be just that. The first hall would contain the upright spirits of those whose names will live on forever in history. . . . The second hall would contain souls adept at turning things to their advantage, including the leaders of the Lin Biao and Jiang Qing counter-revolutionary cliques. . . . The third hall would be for the survivors, those people who did not necessarily harm others, but nor did they oppose tyranny. At the exit a large mirror for self-reflection would be set up with an exhibit of clubs, whips, letters of denunciations, handcuffs as well as various caps like "capitalist roader" and "counter-revolutionary" used to denounce people. This mirror would reflect just what type of soul each individual had. (Barmé 1999:381)

Zhou then points out Ye's alleged appeal to badge collectors to create an "indispensable exhibit" of badges from their collection. Zhou proceeds to discuss what are probably much more factual entreaties to him to continue to lobby for a museum that includes badges. Zhou also quotes in entirety a 1992 article entitled "The Rising Tide of Cultural Revolution Relics" to further make his case for the cultural significance of badges:

So-called Cultural Revolution relics are unique objects that reflect a specific historical period. Chairman Mao quotation songs are one of the inventions of the Cultural Revolution. . . . The shortest line in those songs was "we must combat selfishness and repudiate revisionism" (*yao dousi pixiu*). Although there are only five words it took three minutes to sing. . . . Records of these songs have sold in Hong Kong for as much as H.K. $2500 each. The longest song can't simply be measured in words. At one evening performance called "The Effulgence of Mao Zedong Thought Will Shine through the Ages," the "Three Standard Articles" were put to music and it took a whole night to sing them. The precious red book has also become a commodified artifact that people both in China and overseas have started collecting. The book was produced in over fifty different languages, and, during the Cultural Revolution, some five hundred editions appeared with approximately five billion copies in circulation. If you add to that number the editions produced by various Red Guard groups and revolutionary committees there would have been over ten billion copies in print. But relatively few copies can be found in the cultural relics markets today and prices are constantly on the rise, especially for rare editions. The Mao badge, however, is the most widespread Cultural Revolution product. In the five-year period from the summer of 1966 to the summer of 1971, over ten thousand different designs appeared throughout China with two billion badges in circulation. Overseas Mao badges now sell for anything from U.S. $0.5 to $400. Not long ago, an American-born Chinese bought a Mao badge in the shape of a sunflower for U.S. $500. But Cultural Revolution period stamps have seen the greatest price increase . . .

take, for example, the 1968 stamp "the mountains and rivers of the nation are all red," which was printed incorrectly. In 1988, one of these stamps could fetch six thousand yuan according to the median official price or ten thousand yuan on the open market. All manner of Cultural Revolution relics—lecterns for the works of Chairman Mao, Mao statues, portraits, and various publications—have become the object of collectors' interest.

Zhou finishes his spiel with a prediction: "One can predict with considerable optimism that with the passage of time Mao badges will be appearing among the Chinese antiquities sold at the best international auctions. Similarly, sooner or later Mao badges will find a well-deserved place in the British Museum, the Tokyo Kokuritsu Hakubutsukan, the Met in New York, and the Musee Guimet in Paris."

Worldwide Mao

Indeed, part of Zhou's prediction was accurate. With the help of advances in electronic communications, today peddlers traffic Mao icons to a much broader audience. A pioneer in Internet auctions, eBay provides the most impressive forum for transnational badge exchange. At any given time, eBay lists several hundred Mao items for sale. Badges, or Mao pins, as they are labeled commonly on eBay, represent a significant part of this market. The majority of Mao consumers on eBay are Westerners. Sellers include Westerners, mainland Chinese, and Hong Kong collectors. Prices of Mao badges auctioned range from $2 to $30, with the average bid about $5. Unlike long-time Chinese collectors, eBay sellers auction badges with little or no historical context. Instead, marketing focuses on originality and authenticity, yet ignores any larger context that makes a badge either original or authentic. For example, one seller describes a rather common badge featuring "zhong" as a "unique type." Another seller guarantees that his $20–$40 (opening bid price) anti-Vietnam statuettes made from U.S. aircraft wreckage are "100% authentic and rare." Another Chinese seller goes to some length to hawk a porcelain badge:

> This is an unusual ceramic pin measuring about 1.75 inches in diameter. Mao is in a China People's Liberation Army uniform. The back reads, "Loyal to Chairman Mao Forever—Inner Mongolian Military Region." These pins were issued during the Chinese Cultural Revolution launched by Chinese Communist Party Chairman Mao during his last decade in power (1966–76) to renew the spirit of the Chinese revolution. Most Mao badges were made of cheap metal or plastic. It is most unusual to find a badge made of ceramic, let alone in such perfect condition. This badge is a great representation of this period of history and a great addition to a collection. A must for Cultural Revolution collectors, history buffs or political badge/pin collectors.

Sellers enshroud Mao icons with familiar advertising techniques that connote an urgency and fear of loss. For example, one seller dealing Mao-Nixon Ping Pong paddles warns that "once our supply is gone, these will become quite hard to find again . . . don't miss out," and again at the end, "I have a very limited supply of these, and once they are gone, they are gone!" Another buyer adopts a similar tone to sell a T-shirt with Mao's image: "We found this extremely cool t-shirt at a hip boutique in Bangkok, Thailand. Fantastic image taken straight from a vintage Chinese Cultural Revolution propaganda poster. The colors are rich and the photographic detail is superb. Needless to say, chances are

slim to none that you will ever see such a great top anywhere else."

EBay vendors recontextualize Mao's image in myriad
ways, pushing the ever-expanding emotional and intellectual appeal of Mao. One seller, for example, embeds a Mao
badge in a set of "interesting cause" buttons that includes
abortion rights, freedom for South Africa, anti-nuclear test-
ing, and anti-death penalty. The Mao badge is simple, void
of text, aligned beside the more imposing "why do we kill
people who kill people to show that killing people is wrong?"
Another Western seller peddles a Mao place setting through
her perception of Mao's tyranny:

> This unusual plastic artifact features a cameo of the
> head of the late—not soon enough!—unlamented dic-
> tator of Communist China, Chairman Mao Zedong,
> against a halo of transparent red plastic. There is Chi-
> nese writing on the front and back, and I am told (al-
> though I can't guarantee) this artifact is a place setting
> from a state dinner given by Mao for his provincial
> leaders. I can guarantee this rare piece is from Com-
> munist China, and is in good condition, with just mi-
> nor wear.

Consumers reflect an impressive intellectual and emotional depth in their Mao collection activities. Most collectors admit an emotionally based association with the badges
they collect. One collector, for example, collected badges
and other Chinese memorabilia to learn more about Chinese history for the sake of his adopted Chinese daughter.
Collecting badges is a way of "preserving a little of our
daughter's heritage" to bestow upon her as she grows.
Though many admit to not understanding the entire context of Mao badges, they reflected a substantial knowledge
about the Cultural Revolution. More commonly, Western

collectors recontextualized Mao badges with their own coming of age in the 1960s, as in the following narratives:

> When I was a young teenager, there was a bookstore called the Peking Book House. As near as I can figure it was more or less an official agent of the PRC government, and seemed to be there to cater to people interested in China (this was Nixon-Vietnam era) as well as student radicals. There was nothing undergroundy about it but all it sold was Chinese propaganda: Mao and Marxist books, Chinese periodicals, Mao hats and jackets, posters and Mao badges. It was run by an elderly Chinese man and I don't really recall seeing anybody else in the store. Anyway, I had been brought up to go to peace marches and was very curious about Mao and Marxism. I had written a long term paper on the Long March and in an innocent sort of way thought the Cultural Revolution was really cool. I collected stamps so the Mao badges seemed like a cool adjunct. I wound up buying 5 or ten of them and still have most of them. I also bought red books and bought and wore all the time a blue Mao hat and jacket which in retrospect I'm sure I looked very silly in. Eventually I left the Chicago area for high school, and when I returned to go to college in Chicago in 1976. I remember wearing my Mao badge expecting all fellow students to be doing the same (I surely watched too much TV or something). I wound up being attracted to campus radicals and spent the next ten years being a leftist, wandering in and out of various left-wing sects, though I quickly lost all respect for Maoism when I started examining the ideology with a critical eye. New York City, where I've lived since 1981, has a huge Chinatown (and in earlier days, several pro-Mao radi-

cal bookstores). Though by the 1980s I was no longer a
fan of Mao I still thought the Mao artifacts were kinda
cool, and added slightly to my collection over the years
when I saw something of interest, bringing my collection to something like 25 pins. (For a while off and on
I continued to collect stamps, and loved all the ones
relating to Mao.) When I stumbled onto them on e-Bay
I was very excited. Between shopping on e-Bay, shopping from connections I made on e-Bay, and more
aggressively pursuing vendors in Chinatown and elsewhere, I have increased my collection to several hundred, plus a number of Mao statues, plaques, cups, silk
wall hangings, books, clocks, teapots, etc. I was fascinated by a political icon turned into a religious and
culturally weighted symbol. The irony of Maoism's
alleged atheism producing such a wealth of devotional
ephemera is intriguing to me. As a student of religious
symbolism—I suppose I've replaced my political interests of years past with a series of spiritual explorations—I find the iconography comparable to that of
Catholicism's. In fact I love those cheap plaster saint
statutes and have many of them on a shelf above some
of my Mao statuary at home. Which isn't to say I worship Mao . . . he was a thoroughly despicable character; his liberation of China from the bonds of feudalism
notwithstanding. The cartoony quality of the Cultural
Revolution's propaganda intrigues me as a graphic de-
signer; its religiosity and marketing brilliance attract
me despite the repugnance of its literal message.

Another Western collector similarly relates his interest
in badges to nostalgia:

Mao badges represent a specific time period both in
my life and in the events of that period . . . 1967 through

1971. Not only was China going through its Cultural
Revolution, the US was as well having a real cultural
revolution of its own. It is hard to describe a politically active college campus of that era without having
been there. In addition to the traditional pursuits of
maturing, drinking, socializing, learning, acting out and
chasing girls, there was the tremendous new pressure
. . . the Vietnam War. Not one male student of draft
age that I knew at the time didn't spend lots of time
thinking about this. . . . The reality of the Cold War hit
home. When I speak of the 60s—I am referring to
roughly the period between 1965 (the year US troops
hit Vietnam in large numbers) through 1975 (the fall
of Saigon). Political activism swept the campus, not
only with myriad political rallies and meetings sponsored and initiated by various groups, but even to the
types of clothing worn. Any concrete symbol of one's
political beliefs was often adopted. Mao pins were not
common, but I did see a few being worn. . . . I knew a
fellow who had a huge poster of Mao in his room as
well as Lenin, he was Catholic and yet considered himself a communist. One of his friends, I swear, wore a
black-blue cap similar to Lenin's as well as a Lenin
goatee. In my discussions with him I soon observed
that the Chinese version of the communist model was
the one most often preferred by idealist socialist radi-
cals. The Soviet Union's model was under scrutiny due
to the leaks about the excesses of Stalin and the 1968
crushing of the Czech defiance in Prague. The other
"pure" red spirit was Che Guevara. So, according to
these folks, the hope of Communism was the Chinese,
peasant, model. It is important to remember that China
was still "closed" and media information was not the
best or most accurate. The Cultural Revolution was

described in a very vague way. I remember reading that bodies were spotted floating down the rivers to Hong Kong. They gave no specifics as to what this movement was about or how it was being administered. My attraction to these badges I think is largely nostalgic reminding me of this period of time. Anything political from China was seen as quite exotic and hard to come by. I also collect some Soviet items from this period, certain pins of Lenin, banners, etc. There was a real shock value attached to these items in the 1960s . . . a sort of subliminal message that "the times were a changin'" and that almost anything was possible here in the US's Cultural Revolution as well. Some other attractions to Mao pins revolve around the idea that we are looking at "jewelry with a purpose." Men in our culture do not get a chance to wear much jewelry . . . a tie tack, a watch and not much else, yet the sparkle of gold, silver and rich enamel is often as attractive to guys as well as gals. I also collected and am very knowledgeable about military insignia . . . it too has a jewelry attractiveness and it doesn't challenge the macho prejudice about collecting jewelry as being effeminate. One can also note that military men do get to wear "jewelry" even in quantity as symbols of service and courage. There really isn't a lot of 1965–75 memorabilia around, except in the field of rock music. A few peace signs jewelry, political buttons—Free Angela Davis—Stop the War and the like. This time period doesn't have the style of Deco, Deco Moderne or even Art Nouveau that is reflected in furniture, advertising, etc. So, this is a way to have a legitimate collectible of the 1960s. My attraction to these badges is certainly not one of political approval. If one extrapolates the ideas and tenets of Mao's cultural revolution, you get the genocide of Cambodia. This whole notion of "cleansing" a society of the bourgeoisie and its ideas is abhorrent to me. Mao wanted reeducation, the Pathet Lao said why bother, just shoot them . . . and they did as the world just sat and watched. After graduating from college I kicked around a few years and then returned to college in 1978, to get a degree in journalism. I then worked 10 years as a reporter and an editor, then chucked that all in when I got a chance to support myself with my art. I still have and champion much of my 1960s ways . . . Do your own thing (as long as you're not hurting anybody else); Today is the first day of the rest of your life; Don't trust governments, etc. I am also a male feminist—complete with a photo of myself with Gloria Steinem hanging on the wall. . . . Life's greatest surprise is that I am still here after all that crazy Animal House living I used to do.

In addition to exchanges of Mao propaganda, the Internet boasts a virtual Cultural Revolution museum. The museum introduces the Cultural Revolution with a statement on the unique ability of the World Wide Web to provide a space for remembering the Cultural Revolution:

Many would argue that the Cultural Revolution museum should be located in Beijing, or at least somewhere in China. Indeed, the Beijing government has invested substantial sums in building a western-style opera house. Yet for obvious reasons, the Cultural Revolution museum cannot be established in Beijing or elsewhere in China. Instead, for the moment, the Cultural Revolution museum is located on the internet: a place in the middle of nowhere yet not so far away from anywhere else. During the Cultural Revolution, a popular saying dictated that you should "take things

as they come." Along the same lines, establishing the
Cultural Revolution museum can be seen as the best
solution for the time being. Besides, a virtual Cultural
Revolution museum has many advantages, not the
least of which that you can come and visit it with just
the click of a mouse.

Eating Bitterness: Cultural Revolution Restaurants

The preservation and institutionalization of Mao
badges and the Cultural Revolution appear most prominently in the form of Cultural Revolution theme restaurants. Beijing now boasts several theme restaurants that
re-create the rural atmosphere familiar to former Red Guards
sent to the countryside. One restaurant, Hei Tudi (Black
Earth), advertises: "Toil and sweat in the great Northern
wilderness yesterday; gather in joy in Hei Tudi today." Hei
Tudi features Mao memorabilia on the walls, including
badges and slogans. Rustic dining rooms and northern cuisine evoke a nostalgic atmosphere. A sense of adventure
and martyrdom prevails. Backpacks decorate the walls with
slogans such as "Recall the past, full of eventful years." Pictures of Mao with children and Red Guards working in the
countryside flank charity boxes to sponsor poor rural students. The boxes sit below white notebooks that list children who can't afford to go to school in Shanbei. The writing
on the boxes implores diners to "give your love to the kids
from poverty-stricken areas" and "It only takes sixty yuan
per student per school year!" Laosanjie, another popular
Cultural Revolution theme restaurant, posts a similar advertisement. The Laosanjie Economic Development Company announces contributions to the Shanxi Province Yijan
County Leadership Group of Hope Project to help the poor
and promote education.

Turning Mao into museum fare through theme restaurants and professional exhibits provides a safe realism through which Chinese can reenact the Cultural Revolution. Restaurants neatly order the Cultural Revolution, securing propaganda behind glass. Strategic incongruities with the Cultural Revolution are readily available. Pricey menus (with a variety of choices beyond northern cuisine) and upscale clientele moderate the rustic restaurant atmosphere. At Hei Tudi, prices range from 8 to 400 yuan ($1.50 to $80), the average meal listed at 40 to 50 yuan ($8 to $10). At Laosanjie, the prices are lower, ranging from 10 to 40 yuan ($2 to $5). But the customers offer an impressive array of status symbols, including cellular phones, private automobiles (including, at one sitting, a Mercedes), fashionable clothing, and briefcases. Laosanjie, particularly, suggests a trendy dating spot as young couples share benches for dinner to Western background music, including selections such as "I Am Your Lady; You Are My Man," and "I Can't Live if Living Is without You." The more popular theme dishes include "nostalgic bites" such as cornmeal cake, northeast corn maize gruel, and Xian mutton bread soup. "Reunion dinners" include choices such as the "party of heroes" and "longevity and harvest."

Particularly telling traces of the new Chinese political economy within the setting of the Cultural Revolution restaurants are the selected Mao quotations, such as "Stay busy, you'll have solid food; stay idle, you'll have to drink soup." Business cards and advertisements swamp bulletin boards in response to the invitation to "find your old battle companion" and "make new friends."

Singapore's newly opened House of Mao represents the most striking culinary bastardization of the Cultural Revolution. An upscale eatery, the House of Mao is elaborately decorated with Cultural Revolution memorabilia. The

"Great Hall" presents an area for dining designed after the Great Hall of the People, complete with an eighteen-person table under a Chairman Mao portrait. An outdoor terrace, paved to resemble Tiananmen Square, provides a more syncretic atmosphere combining traditional Chinese music and disco. A back bar presents muted footage on Mao and the Cultural Revolution, and bathroom stalls represent jail cells. Waiters dress in Red Guard fashion and distribute menus fashioned as Little Red Books. Owners plan a second House of Mao, to be opened in London.

The epitome of the museumification of Mao, his body itself, locked in crystal, offers an equivalent security, with further privileges impossible during the Cultural Revolution: confronting Mao. Visitors see Mao, walk by him with warnings not to overstep the boundary drawn around the body. The comforts of capitalism are, literally, right around the corner, as visitors exit into a swamp of Mao trinkets as well as toy and gift shops unrelated to the mausoleum.

Rebirth

The most recent trend of Mao's revival reflects perhaps the greatest liberty with or from the Cultural Revolution of all: the opportunity to become Mao. Discussing her interview with collector Wang Anting, Li (1993) comments on the contentedness and calmness Wang evokes, what she describes as her feeling that there was something unusual about him. Visitors describe him as immortal, wise, and uncommon. One visitor reaches the inevitable conclusion: "All he has in his heart is Chairman Mao. He dreams about Chairman Mao in the evening, all the time. When I look at his expression when he talks, something always reminds me of Mao Zedong."

Mao look-alikes have also found increasing profitability in their resemblance to the Chairman, commenting on their growing numbers of job offers and groupies (McGregor 1993). Gu Yue, the best-known Mao look-alike, describes a transcendence when playing Mao. He reports that he begins to walk differently, view history differently, and he smokes. Another Mao look-alike criticizes Gu for trying to become Mao at the same time that he describes his own transcendence in role-playing Mao.

Lin's Back In: Faking the Revolution

Historical memory and modernity collide yet again in the commonplace reproductions of Mao icons. Manufacturers replicate the famous statue featuring Lin Biao and Mao to meet the market demand for Lin Biao icons, valuable after the massive destruction of his image following his fall from power. Sellers target Western consumers with these reproductions, as is evident by their placement in the market: lavish tourist hotels (and surrounding shops) and antique markets advertising in English. The replicas are representative of what Picard (1995) identifies as "boundary maintenance," in which producers reserve a distinct product for outsiders. However, the fact that the Chinese also consume Mao relics complicates a simplistic commentary on Western tourist gullibility.

The Mao replicas manufactured in China for tourists skew history in subtle ways. Mao and Lin Biao reproductions sport untarnished Lins, unlike the Cultural Revolution propaganda featuring Lin's conspicuous absence. Since images of Lin typically include Mao, the wholesale destruction of these icons was not an option; instead, individuals rubbed off, marked over, or erased Lin, leaving an infamous shadow.

Badge reproductions are strikingly anonymous, typically featuring a generic image of an elderly Mao devoid of any surrounding visual design or writing. The richly symbolic text characteristic of Cultural Revolution badges is absent.

Chinese vendors are attuned to Western desire for authenticity, and reproductions (and the marketing strategies to hawk them) have become more sophisticated. Admiring a set of perfectly groomed Mao statues one day in the market, I asked the vendor if the statues were new. He insisted they were very old. I pressed the issue, and he detailed aspects of the statue with reference to Cultural Revolution history. Finally, I coyly explained that I was not interested in old statues; I told him that I wanted a new one. The vendor eyed me quizzically and distrustfully, then instantly produced an identical statue to the right, claiming that this was the new one. In another instance, I was looking at one of the very popular Mao lighters that blare "East Is Red." The vendor approached, assuring me that the lighter was old. I knew that the lighters were not Cultural Revolution products and protested, hoping to solicit more information from him. However, he didn't waver; instead, he pointed out all of the scratches on the product.

The revival of Mao image consumption reflects the desire among both Chinese and Westerners to "return to the primitive" that characterizes tourists' desires in Third World countries (Bruner and Kirshenblatt-Gimblett 1994). Representations of the Cultural Revolution allow tourists to mingle with the sanitized yet savage era through Mao relics and retire in the luxury of economic reform. The irony, of course, is that the pilgrimage to the depths of China's historical underbelly is, in reality, remarkably shallow.

Mao Consumption and Chinese Identity

Western media are exceptionally attentive to the resurgence of Mao in contemporary China. However, that
attention too often adopts a patronizing tone, wavering between the dual temptations to sell China as a nation of hero-
seekers and capitalist wannabes who are selling Mao in the
pursuit of Westernization. The historical burden of the chaotic Cultural Revolution serves as an ever-ready reference
point for the Chinese nation's naiveté. The modus operandi
for Western renderings of Mao's revival appears to be representations emphasizing the irony of Mao's endurance as a
cultural and national symbol. The suggestion that Westerners understand the irony in all their global wisdom reigns,
with little attempt to accord the Chinese that same benefit.
With increased sophistication, the Chinese are establishing
an eclectic national identity in the modern world. Of course,
ironic consumption rituals are by no means unique to the
Chinese; however, Western intrigue with socialist kitsch is
simply read as eclectic humor.

The contemporary Mao revival resists an essentialized
Chinese national identity. With an increasingly diversified
symbolic potential, Mao continues to be invoked as a bro-
ker between past and present ideals and agendas for a Chinese nationalist ideology. As with most nations, a new
Chinese nationalist ideology cannot afford to ignore the past.
The Chinese pilgrimage to the past offers an opportunity to
formalize Mao as a middleman between history and global
modernity. The endurance of Mao as icon insists on an ex-
periential engagement with the past that is at once creative,
dynamic, and critical. The reenactment of Mao and the Cultural Revolution keeps the lessons of the past visible and
tangible. The theater of contemporary Mao consumption is
necessarily selective but privileged with a playfulness that
dodges centralized control. Though the Mao phenomenon

is rife with ironies, these ironies are not Western amusements enjoyed by clumsy capitalists. Instead, the contemporary consumption of Mao reflects a semiotic syncretism that indigenizes economic reform and transnational interactions. Mao's image continues to be implicated in the making of social relationships, although the connections forged have an increasingly global flavor. Vendors, students, and collectors alike understand the national and transnational appeal and ambiguity of Mao's image. The genius in keeping Mao around, in all his irony, is his efficacy in negotiating socioeconomic reform as much as the cultural and historical legacy that preceded it.

In endeavoring to write a biography of Mao badges, I am in the unique position of coming to a conclusion about a career that is in full swing. Late in my second research trip, I chased down a young female student who was walking down the street with a small Mao badge pinned to her chest. I asked her why she was wearing the badge. She shrugged, giggled, and then offered me the badge. I stood, staring at her, racking my brain for a better way to ask her why she was wearing the badge. The incident offered a unique transnational moment: the anthropologist, confronting modernity in its most ambiguous form, and a young Chinese woman, signifying, but hesitating to define the riddle of that modernity—a theatrical drama that conflates a legacy of ritually defined social order, the political fallout of Mao's reign, and experimentation with global economics through the relentless prism of Mao's image.

References

Aijmer, Goran. 1996. Political Ritual: Aspects of the Mao Cult during the Cultural Revolution. *China Information* 11 (2/3):215.

Anagnost, Ann. 1997. *National Past-Times: Narrative, Representation, and Power in Modern China.* Durham, N.C.: Duke University Press.

———. 1985. Hegemony and the Improvisation of Resistance: Political Culture and Popular Practice in Contemporary China. Ph.D. dissertation, University of Michigan.

Anderson, Benedict. 1983. *Imagined Communities: Reflections on the Origins and Spread of Nationalism.* New York: Verso.

Andrews, Julia. 1994. *Painters and Politics in the People's Republic of China, 1949–1979.* Berkeley: University of California Press.

Appadurai, Arjun. 1990. Disjuncture and Difference in the Global Cultural Economy. *Public Culture* 2 (2):1–24.

———, ed. 1992. *The Social Life of Things: Commodities in Cultural Perspective.* Cambridge, U.K.: Cambridge University Press.

Barmé, Geremie R. 1999. *In the Red: On Contemporary Chinese Culture.* New York: Columbia University Press.

———. 1996. *Shades of Mao: The Posthumous Cult of the Great Leader.* Armonk, N.Y.: M. E. Sharpe.

Barnouin, Barbara, and Yu Changgen. 1993. *Ten Years of Turbulence: The Chinese Cultural Revolution.* New York: Kegan Paul International.

Basket of Fruit. 1968. *Peking Review* 32, August 9.

Benewick, Robert. 1999. Icons of Power: Mao Zedong and the Cultural Revolution. In *Picturing Power in the People's Republic: Posters of the Cultural Revolution,* ed. Harriet Evans and Stephanie Donald. New York: Rowman and Littlefield.

———. 1995. Badgering the People: A Retrospective, 1949–1995. In *Belief in China.* London: Brighton Green Foundation.

Bennett, Gordon, and Ronald Montaperto. 1972. *Red Guard: The Political Biography of Dai Hsiao-ai.* Garden City, N.Y.: Anchor Books.

Berger, Dorian. 1997. *The Red Book and the Power Structure of Communist China.* http://www.sspp.net.

Bishop, Bill. 1996. *"Badges of Chairman Mao Zedong." http://www. cind.org/CR/Maobadge/index.html.*

Bishop, Robert. 1989. *Qilai! Mobilizing One Billion Chinese: The Chinese Communication System.* Ames: Iowa State University Press.

Bruner, Edward. 1996. Tourism in Ghana: The Representation of Slavery and the Return of the Black Diaspora. *American Anthropologist* 98 (2):290–304.

Bruner, Edward, and Barbara Kirshenblatt-Gimblett. 1994. Maasai on the Lawn: Tourist Realism in East Africa. *Cultural Anthropology* 9:435–470.

Carry the Great Proletarian Cultural Revolution to the End. 1966. Peking: Foreign Languages Press.

Chairman Mao Swims in the Yangtze. 1966. *Peking Review* 31, July, 29.

Chan, Anita. 1985. *Children of Mao: Personality Development and Political Activism in the Red Guard Movement.* Seattle: University of Washington Press.

——— 1992. Dispelling Misconceptions about the Red Guard Movement: The Necessity to Re-examine Cultural Revolution Factionalism and Periodization. *Journal of Contemporary China* 1 (1):61–85.

Chan, Anita, Stanley Rosen, and Jonathan Unger. 1980. Students and Class Warfare: The Social Roots of the Red Guard Conflict in Guangzhou (Canton). *China Quarterly* 83:397–446.

Chan Waifong. 1994. Giant Mao Statue Goes under Hammer Abroad. *South China Morning Post,* November 3,10.

Chang, Jung. 1991. *Wild Swans: Three Daughters of China.* Garden City, N.Y.: Anchor Books.

Chen, Jack. 1975. *Inside the Cultural Revolution.* New York: Macmillan.

Chen, Yungsheng. 1971. *Brutalities Committed by the Red Guards.* Taipan, Taiwan: Li Ming Culture Service Center.

Chu, Godwin. 1979. The Current Structure and Functions of China's Mass Media. In Chu and Hsu, *Moving a Mountain,* 57–75.

———, ed. 1978. *Popular Media in China: Shaping New Cultural Patterns.* Honolulu: University Press of Hawaii.

Chu, Godwin, and Ai-li Chin. 1978. Cultural Processes in China: Continuity and Change. In Chu, *Popular Media in China,* 222–248.

———, and Francis Hsu, eds. 1979. *Moving a Mountain: Cultural Change in China.* Honolulu: University Press of Hawaii.

Chu, Leonard. 1978. Sabers and Swords for the Chinese Children: Revolutionary Children's Folk Songs. In Chu, *Popular Media in China,* 16–50.

Chuang, HC. 1967. *The Great Proletarian Cultural Revolution: A Terminological Study.* Berkeley: Studies in Chinese Communist Terminology no. 12.

Douglas, Mary, and Baron Isherwood. 1989. *The World of Goods: Towards an Anthropology of Consumption*. New York: Basic Books.

Dutton, Michael. 1998. *Streetlife China*. Cambridge: Cambridge University Press.

Errington, Frederick, and Deborah Gewertz. 1996. The Individuation of Tradition in Papua New Guinean Modernity. *American Anthropologist* 98 (1):114–126.

Errington, Shelly. 1998. *The Death of Authentic Primitive Art and Other Tales of Progress*. Berkeley: University of California Press.

Esherick, Joseph, and Jeffrey Wasserstrom. 1994. Acting out Democracy: Political Theater in Modern China. In Wasserstrom and Perry, *Popular Protest and Political Culture in Modern China*, 32–70.

Evans, Harriet, and Stephanie Donald. 1999. *Picturing Power in the People's Republic: Posters of the Cultural Revolution*. New York: Rowman and Littlefield.

Feng Jicai. 1985. *Chysanthemums and Other Stories*. San Diego: Harcourt Brace Jovanovich.

——— 1991. *Voices from the Whirlwind: An Oral History of the Chinese Cultural Revolution*. New York: Pantheon.

Friedman, Edward. 1994. Democracy and "Mao Fever." *Journal of Contemporary China* 6:84–95.

Gao Yuan. 1987. *Born Red: A Chronicle of the Cultural Revolution*. Stanford, Calif.: Stanford University Press.

Gold, Thomas. 1989. Guerrilla Interviewing among the *Getihu*. In Link et al., *Unofficial China*, 175–192.

Gray, Sherry. 1992. Bombard the Headquarters: Local Politics and Citizen Participation in the Great Proletarian Cultural Revolution and the 1989 Movement in Shenyang. Ph.D. diss., University of Denver.

Hannerz, Ulf. 1989. Notes on the Global Ecumene. *Public Culture* 1 (2):66–75.

Hobsbawm, Eric, and Terence Ranger, eds. 1983. *The Invention of Tradition*. Cambridge: Cambridge University Press.

Hong Yung Lee. 1979. Mao's Strategy for Revolutionary Change: A Case Study of the Cultural Revolution. *China Quarterly* 77:50–73.

———. 1978. *The Politics of the Chinese Cultural Revolution: A Case Study*. Berkeley: University of California Press.

Howes, David. 1996. *Cross-Cultural Consumption: Global Markets, Local Realities*. New York: Routledge.

Hwang, John. 1978. *Lien Huan Hua*. In Chu, *Popular Media in China*, 51–72.

Jarman, Neil. 1997. *Material Conflicts: Parades and Visual Displays in Northern Ireland*. Oxford and London: Berg.

Jones, Andrew. 1994. The Politics of Popular Music in Post-Tiananmen China. In Wasserstrom and Perry, *Popular Protest and Political Culture in Modern China*, 148–166.

Kearney, Michael. 1995. The Local and the Global: The Anthropology of Globalization and Transnationalism. *Annual Review of Anthropology* 24:547–565.

Kirshenblatt-Gimblett, Barbara. 1998. *Destination Culture: Tourism, Museums, and Heritage.* Berkeley: University of California Press.

Kopytoff, Igor. 1992. The Cultural Biography of Things: Commoditization as Process. In Appadurai, *The Social Life of Things.*

Kraus, Richard. 1991. *Brushes with Power: Modern Politics and the Chinese Art of Calligraphy.*

Landsberger, Stefan. 1996. Mao as the Kitchen God: Religious Aspects of the Mao Cult during the Cultural Revolution. *China Information* 11 (2/3):196–214.

———. 1995. *Chinese Propaganda Posters: From Revolution to Modernization.* Armonk, N.Y.: M. E. Sharpe.

Lanfant, Marie-Françoise et al., eds. 1995. *International Tourism: Identity and Change.* London: Sage.

Leijonhufvud, Goran. 1990. *Going against the Tide: On Dissent and Big-Character Posters in China.* London: Curzon Press.

Li Xuemi. 1993. *Mao Zedong Xiangzhang Shoucang Yu Jianshang* (Mao Zedong Badges: Collection and Connoisseurship). Beijing: Guoji Wenhua Chuban She.

Li Zhisui. 1994. *The Private Life of Chairman Mao.* New York: Random House.

Liang Heng and Judith Shapiro. 1983. *Son of the Revolution.* New York: Vintage Books.

Lin Biao, on the study of Mao's works. 1970. *Important Documents on the Great Proletarian Cultural Revolution in China.* Peking: Foreign Languages Press.

Ling, Ken. 1972. *Red Guard: From Schoolboy to "Little General" in Mao's China.* London: Macdonald.

Link, Perry, Richard Madsen, and Paul Pickowicz, eds. 1989. *Unofficial China: Popular Culture and Thought in the People's Republic of China.* Boulder, Colo.: Westview Press.

Linnekin, Jocelyn. 1992. On the Theory and Politics of Cultural Construction in the Pacific. *Oceania* 62:249–263.

Lu, Xiuyuan. 1994. A Step toward Understanding Popular Violence in China's Cultural Revolution. *Pacific Affairs* 67 (4):533–564.

Lubman, Sarah. 1991. Chinese Man Devotes Life to Mania for Mao. *San Francisco Examiner,* March 1, A8.

Luo, Ziping. 1990. *A Generation Lost: China under the Cultural Revolution.* New York: Henry Holt.

Ma, Bo. 1995. *Blood Red Sunset: A Memoir of the Chinese Cultural Revolution.* New York: Penguin Books.

Madsen, Richard. 1984. *Morality and Power in a Chinese Village.* Berkeley: University of California Press.

Magic Mirrors That Show Up All Monsters. 1966. *People's Daily,* June 20.

McCracken, Grant. 1988. *Culture and Consumption*. Bloomington: Indiana University Press.

McGregor, James. 1993. On and Off the Screen, China's Big Star Plays Mao Zedong to a T. *Wall Street Journal*, June 29, A1.

Meisner, Maurice. 1977. *Mao's China: A History of the People's Republic*. New York: Free Press.

Miller, Daniel. 1987. *Material Culture and Mass Consumption*. Cambridge: Blackwell.

———, ed. 1998. *Material Cultures: Why Some Things Matter*. Chicago: University of Chicago Press.

Mintz, Sidney. 1985. *Sweetness and Power: The Place of Sugar in Modern History*. New York: Penguin Books.

Niu-Niu. 1995. *No Tears for Mao: Growing Up in the Cultural Revolution*. Chicago: Academy Chicago Publishers.

Noth, J. Wolfger Pohlmann, and Kai Resche, eds. 1991. *China Avant-Garde: Counter-Currents in Art and Culture*. Hong Kong: Oxford University Press.

One Hundred Items for Destroying the Old and Establishing the New: Beijing Number 26 Middle School Red Guards. 1970. *Chinese Sociology and Anthropology: A Journal of Translations* 2 (3–4), Spring–Summer:215.

Orlove, Benjamin, ed. 1997. *The Allure of the Foreign: Imported Goods in Postcolonial Latin America*. Ann Arbor: University of Michigan Press.

Painting Pictures of Chairman Mao Is Our Greatest Happiness. 1968. *China Reconstructs*, October, 2.

Peoples of the World Love Chairman Mao. 1968. *China Reconstructs*, March, 26.

Perry, Elizabeth. 1994. Introduction. In Wasserstrom and Perry, *Popular Protest and Political Culture in Modern China*, 1–14.

Picard, Michel. 1995. Cultural Heritage and Tourist Capital: Cultural Tourism in Bali. In Lanfant et al., *International Tourism*, 44–66.

Poon, David Jim-tat. 1978. Tatzepao: Its History and Significance as a Communication Medium. In Godwin Chu, ed., *Popular Media in China*. Honolulu: University of Hawaii Press.

Pye, Lucian. 1979. Communication and Political Culture in China. In Chu and Hsu, *Moving a Mountain*, 153–178.

Revolutionary Tapestries Loved by the Millions. 1968. *China Reconstructs*, July, 31.

Saich, Tony. 1990. When Worlds Collide: The Beijing People's Movement of 1989. In *The Chinese People's Movement: Perspectives on Spring 1989*, ed. Tony Saich, 25–49.

Samples of Red Guard Publications II. 1967. Washington, D.C.: U.S. Department of Commerce.

Scharping, Thomas. 1994. The Man, the Myth, the Message—New

Trends in Mao-Literature from China. *China Quarterly* 137:168–179.

Schell, Orville. 1994. *Mandate of Heaven: A New Generation of Entrepreneurs, Dissidents, Bohemians, and Technocrats Lay Claim to China's Future.* New York: Simon and Schuster.

Schmetzer, Uli. 1993. "Sell, Sell, Sell" Is the Latest Saying for Chairman Mao on His Centenary. *Chicago Tribune,* November 21, 7.

Schoenhals, Michael. 1996. *China's Cultural Revolution 1966–1969: Not a Dinner Party.* Armonk, N.Y.: M. E. Sharpe.

———. 1992. *Doing Things with Words in Chinese Politics: Five Studies.* Berkeley: University of California Press.

Schram, Stuart. 1994. Mao Zedong a Hundred Years on: The Legacy of a Ruler. *China Quarterly* 137:125–143.

Schrift, Melissa, and Keith Pilkey. 1996. Revolution Remembered: Chairman Mao and Chinese Nationalist Ideology. *Journal of Popular Culture* 30 (2):169–198.

Schwarcz, Vera. 1991. No Solace from Lethe: History, Memory, and Cultural Identity in Twentieth-Century China. *Daedalus* 120 (2):85–112.

Simmel, George. 1904. Fashion. *International Quarterly* 10:130–155.

Snow, Edgar. 1973. *Red Star Over China.* New York: Grove Press.

Sun-Childers, Jaia, and Douglas Childers. 1996. *The White-Haired Girl.* New York: Picador.

Turner, Victor. 1974. *Dramas, Fields, and Metaphors.* Ithaca, N.Y.: Cornell University Press.

Wasserstrom, Jeffrey. 1991. The Languages of Student Protest. In *Student Protests in Twentieth-Century China,* ed. Jeffrey Wasserstrom, 200–239. Stanford, Calif.: Stanford University Press.

Wasserstrom, Jeffrey, and Elizabeth Perry, eds. 1994. *Popular Protest and Political Culture in Modern China.* Boulder, Colo.: Westview.

Watson, James. 1998. *Golden Arches East: McDonald's in East Asia.* Stanford, Calif.: Stanford University Press.

———. 1993. Rites or Beliefs? The Construction of a Unified Culture in Late Imperial China. In *China's Quest for National Identity,* ed. Lowell Dittmer and Samuel Kim, 80–103. Ithaca, N.Y.: Cornell University Press.

Weiner, Annette. 1992. *Inalienable Possessions: The Paradox of Keeping While Giving.* Berkeley: University of California Press.

Weiner, Annette, and Jane Schneider, eds. 1989. *Cloth and Human Experience.* Washington, D.C.: Smithsonian Institution Press.

Wen Chihua. 1995. *The Red Mirror: Children of China's Cultural Revolution.* Boulder, Colo.: Westview Press.

White, Lynn. 1979. Local Newspapers and Community Change, 1949–1969. In Chu and Hsu, *Moving a Mountain,* 76–112.

White, Robert A. 1994. Mao Badges of the Cultural Revolution: Political Image and Social Upheaval. *International Social Science Review,* 69, nos. 3 & 4: 53–70.

Williams, Rosalind. 1982. *Dream Worlds: Mass Consumption in Late Nineteenth-Century France*. Berkeley: University of California Press.

World's People Eagerly Seek Chairman Mao Badges. 1968. *China Reconstructs* 17 (5):2–4.

Wu, David. 1991. The Construction of Chinese and Non-Chinese Identities. *Daedalus* 120 (2):159–180.

Xu, Ren. 1993. *A Wealth of Learning with Joy: An Album of Mao Zedong Badges*. Shaanxi, China: Shaanxi Tourism Publishing House.

Yan Jiaqi and Gao Gao. 1996. *Turbulent Decade: A History of the Cultural Revolution*. Honolulu: University of Hawaii Press.

Yang, Mayfair Mei-hui. 1994. *Gifts, Favors and Banquets: The Art of Social Relationships in China*. Ithaca, N.Y.: Cornell University Press.

Yang, Rae. 1997. *Spider Eaters: A Memoir*. Berkeley: University of California Press.

Young, Ernest. 1994. Imagining the Ancien Régime in the Deng Era. In Wasserstrom and Perry, *Popular Protest and Political Culture in Modern China*, 18–31.

Yu, Frederick. 1979. China's Mass Communication in Historical Perspective. In Chu and Hsu, *Moving a Mountain*. Honolulu: University of Hawaii Press.

Zhai, Zhenhua. 1992. *Red Flower of China*. New York: Soho Press.

Zhang Lijia and Calum MacLeod. 1999. *China Remembers*. New York: Oxford University Press.

Zhou, Jihou. 1993. *Mao Zedong Xiangzhang Zhi Mi: Shijie Dijiu Da Qiguan* (The Ninth Wonder of the World: The Mystery of the Mao Badge). Taiyuan: Beiyue Wenyi Chuban She.

Index

Aijmer, Goran, 122
Anagnost, Ann, 156
Anderson, Benedict, 12
Andrews, Julia, 89–92
Appadurai, Arjun, 4, 10–11, 25, 119, 151

Ba Jin, 183–185
badge factories: Red Flag, 66; Shanghai United, 66; Shaoshan Mao, 68
badge materials, 70; aluminum, 70–71; American aircraft wreckage, 112, 140; porcelain, 70–72, 189, fig. 3; tin, 61
badge production and consumption: acquisition by "inviting" rather than purchase, 110, 146, 167; calls to cease production of, 71–72; as cultural relics, 178–188; devotion to, 9, 58; disposal of, following Cultural Revolution, 157–158; distinctive, 111–116; esthetic appeal of, 137; exchange of, 110, 112, 113, 142–147, 150, 170; fear of going out without, 129–130; and *guanxi* [connections],151–154; Internet

sales of, 188; mistreatment of, 131–133; pinned to flesh, 58, 114, 115; as political capital, 105–111; pro-democracy movement and, 159; as revolutionary "souvenirs" 114; as shields, 135, 137; trading markets in during Cultural Revolution, 147, 149–151
badge themes: anomalies in, 101–103, figs. 13, 14; "Chairman Mao Goes to Anyuan," 91–95, fig. 10; colors used, 71; commemorative, 116; Dadu River, 87, fig. 9; Deng Xioping, 158, fig. 17; Great Helmsman, fig. 5; Long March, 87; Mao facing right, fig. 13; Mao reviewing Red Guards, 90; Mao with Lin Biao, 82, 83; Mao with Marx, Engels, Lenin, and Stalin, 60, fig. 16; Mao with Zhou Enlai, 83; Mao with Zhu De, 61; Mao's gift of mangoes, 96–99, fig. 4; Mao's global leadership, 85, fig. 12; Mao's writings/calligraphy, 85, 90, fig. 6; May Seventh schools, fig. 11; Peking

About the Author

Melissa Schrift is an assistant professor of anthropology at Middle Tennessee State University.